IMAGES
of America

FORT HANCOCK

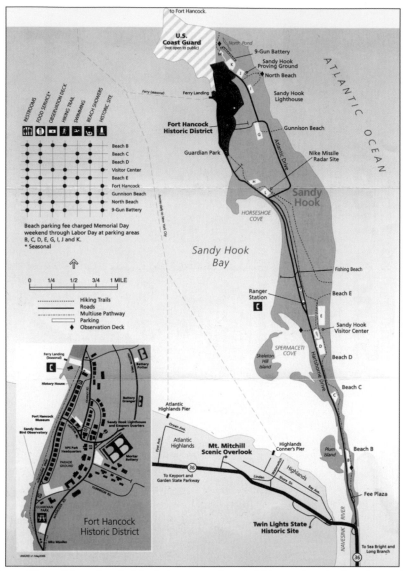

SANDY HOOK UNIT MAP. Sandy Hook is currently a 2,044-acre barrier beach peninsula that stretches over six and a half miles into lower New York Harbor. For many years, the U.S. Army used Sandy Hook to defend the harbor area, but with changing times, the peninsula eventually became a public park. During 1974–1975, most of Sandy Hook became part of Gateway National Recreation Area, and since then an average of more than 2 million visitors a year enjoy its natural areas and historic sites that include Sandy Hook Lighthouse and Fort Hancock, the last army fort at Sandy Hook. (National Park Service.)

On the cover: **EARLY FORT HANCOCK SOLDIERS.** Armed with Krag Jorgensen rifles and wearing army uniforms from the Spanish-American War period, a group of soldiers stationed at Fort Hancock strike a war-like pose for the camera around 1899–1900. The photograph was probably taken in the forested area located southeast of the fort's enlisted men's barracks where soldiers conducted maneuvers and pitched tent encampments between the late 1890s and the early 1940s. It also might have been taken during what is today usually referred to as "war games," but back then was called a "sham battle." (Sandy Hook Unit.)

IMAGES
of America

FORT HANCOCK

Thomas Hoffman

ARCADIA
PUBLISHING

Published by Arcadia Publishing
Charleston SC, Chicago IL, Portsmouth NH, San Francisco CA

Printed in the United States of America

Library of Congress Catalog Card Number: 2007923585

For all general information contact Arcadia Publishing at:
Telephone 843-853-2070
Fax 843-853-0044
E-mail sales@arcadiapublishing.com
For customer service and orders:
Toll-Free 1-888-313-2665

Visit us on the Internet at www.arcadiapublishing.com

*This book is dedicated to all the military personnel
and civilians who lived, worked, and served at Fort Hancock
and created the post's great military legacy, and also to
my children, Andrew, Kevin, and Becky, who, by
growing up among the fort's old buildings and gun batteries,
developed a deep interest in our nation's history.*

CONTENTS

ACKNOWLEDGMENTS

I have always felt that whenever anyone reads a book they should always read the author's acknowledgements, simply because authors are inspired, encouraged, and supported by other people that help them to write their books. Without these special people, an author doesn't get the book written, and any writer, especially a historian, is not worth his or her salt unless they acknowledge the help and support of others. So I would like to thank local Monmouth County historians, the late Howard K. Hayden, George H. Moss Jr., the late Samuel Stelle Smith, and former National Park Service chief historian Edwin C. Bearss, for inspiring me to research the history of Sandy Hook when I arrived to work and live there, and also local historians Randall Gabrielan and John P. King for encouraging me to write a history about Fort Hancock. I am extremely grateful and indebted to those who provided photographs and graphics when I asked for their help, including Karin and Bruce Stocking of the W. S. Hancock Society; Mark A. Berhow, a consummate historian and expert on the history of American coast artillery and Nike missile defenses; Bolling Smith and Greg Hagge, expert coast artillery historians; and archivist Alicia Mauldin-Ware, and reference librarian Alan Aimone, both at the U.S. Military Academy, West Point, New York.

My special thanks to Mary Trocchia Rasa, National Park Service museum curator at Sandy Hook, who worked very hard to provide copies of many of the historic images that appear in this book, and Janet Kurka, for providing the Sandy Hook Unit and Gateway maps. I must thank my family for helping me write this book, including my daughter, Rebecca Hoffman, and her friend Amber Venchenco, for picking out those historic photographs they found to be the most interesting; to my son Kevin Hoffman, without whom I could not have written this book; and to my mother, Anne M. Hoffman, who helped me financially to reproduce many of the photographs for this book. Lastly, a special thank you goes to Arcadia Publishing and editor Dawn Robertson for making this book a reality to be enjoyed by all who read it.

Images in this volume are courtesy of Aberdeen Proving Ground (APG), author's collection (AC), Mark A. Berhow (MB), National Archives (NA), National Park Service (NPS), Sandy Hook Unit (SHU), Service of Coast Artillery; Hines and Ward (SCA), Karen and Bruce Stocking (KBS), and West Point Archives (WPA).

INTRODUCTION

Today Sandy Hook is a well-known, very popular, and much visited park that is part of Gateway National Recreation Area. The sands of this barrier beach peninsula are important to American maritime and military history because of Sandy Hook's geographical location. Fronting on the Atlantic Ocean at the entrance to lower New York Harbor just 19 miles south of Battery Park at the southern tip of Manhattan Island, Sandy Hook's natural location at the harbor's entrance made it an important navigational landmark and also a strategic defense site that protected New York City and its vicinity.

From the 1600s to the early 1900s, all large ships entering and leaving New York Harbor had to use a narrow curving channel located around the northern tip of Sandy Hook. Ships had to sail very close to Sandy Hook using the Sandy Hook ship channel, and this is what made the area such a strategically important site in defending the harbor from enemy warships. Since the American Revolution, different types of fortifications have occupied Sandy Hook in times of war and peace. Each fort represented a new defense system that reflected the latest technological advances in weapons, fort construction, and tactics. The different generations of forts built at Sandy Hook culminated with Fort Hancock, which would prove to be the longest serving, most extensive, and most fortified fort ever built on Sandy Hook.

Sandy Hook's strategic value was recognized long before Fort Hancock was established, when in 1687, Thomas Dongan, New York's British governor, suggested that "a small Fort with twelve guns [be built] upon Sandy Hook, the Channel there being so near the shore that no vessel can go in nor out, but . . . must come so near the Point that from on board one might too a biscuit cake on shore." It is not known whether this fort was ever built, but the first known fortification of Sandy Hook definitely took place during the American Revolution. The British navy and army fortified Sandy Hook with temporary shore batteries after the Battle of Monmouth in 1778 when a French fleet showed up off the south end of the peninsula and threatened to sail into the harbor. The French fleet decided not to attack and sailed away, but Sandy Hook proved its strategic value in wartime.

During the War of 1812, many temporary fortifications were built in and around New York City before and during the war. This included Fort Gates, a wooden bastioned fort that was located north of Sandy Hook Lighthouse overlooking the tip of Sandy Hook. The War of 1812 proved to the young United States that it needed to protect its vast maritime frontier with a permanent and well-planned system of harbor defense forts. This included construction of a pentagon-shaped granite masonry fort at Sandy Hook, which was constructed between 1859 and 1867. Officially referred to as the "Fort at Sandy Hook," the fort was never completed because it and all masonry forts were made obsolete by the introduction of rifled artillery during the Civil War.

A revolution in arms development, and even an international arms race, was spawned by the American Civil War. During 1885 and 1886, Pres. Grover Cleveland appointed his secretary of war, William C. Endicott, to chair a special board to review America's entire coastal defense system and make recommendations for improvements. The board's recommendations led to the refortifying of 23 of America's key coastal areas using the latest types of guns emplaced in the newest type of fortification, the concrete gun battery. The Endicott System of harbor defense also included a "Submarine Mine Defense System," which were electrically controlled underwater minefields placed out in harbors during wartime.

Starting in 1888, Congress made appropriations for coastal defense such as constructing mine casemates, which were the command centers that underwater mines were detonated from via electric cables. This included the conversion of the southwest bastion of the old Civil War "Fort at Sandy Hook" into a mine casemate in 1890, making it one of the first five mine casemates in the Endicott System of harbor defense. Sandy Hook was also chosen as the site to build America's first new prototype gun batteries of the Endicott System: Lift-Gun Battery No. 1 (later designated Battery Potter) and the Sandy Hook Mortar Battery. This led to "the fortifications at Sandy Hook [being] designated as Fort Hancock, in Honor of the late Maj. Gen. Winfield Scott Hancock" by the war department on October 30, 1895.

The army planned to build more gun batteries at Fort Hancock, but it also knew that there were no support structures to house the many soldiers needed to man Fort Hancock's defenses. To rectify this situation, the Army Quartermaster Corps took great pains to layout and design a spacious, comfortable post for soldiers to live and work in. Detailed plans were made during 1896 for what would essentially be a town located behind but near the fort's gun batteries. The fort was not like the centuries-old concept of walled fortresses, but was an open, town-like area, with most of the buildings made of buff (yellow) brick, which was a better quality, though more expensive grade of brick to withstand Sandy Hook's harsh maritime environment.

The army believed that the post could be built during 1897, but a variety of frustrating factors delayed the completion of the fort's first 38 buildings until late in 1899. Like many civilian towns, Fort Hancock also grew, with more buff brick and some wooden buildings being added to the post between 1900 and 1910. The fort's defenses also expanded and included some unique ones in the history of American fortifications, including the nine-gun battery, built between 1897 and 1902, and Battery Arrowsmith, Fort Hancock's last counterweight disappearing gun battery built between 1907 and 1909. Of all the army's gun batteries built to defend American harbors from 1890 to 1945, there was only one that mounted nine disappearing guns, and there was probably only one gun battery that was built to defend the rear area behind an American harbor defense fort. Also some of the first searchlights for locating warships at night, and range-finding stations for accurately locating warships employed at United States harbor defense forts were located at Fort Hancock.

During the early 1900s, troops stationed at other New York harbor defense forts came to Fort Hancock to conduct their annual target practice, and the fort also hosted the senior class of West Point cadets. During World War I and World War II, the fort expanded greatly with many wooden, standard-designed barracks, mess halls, and other support buildings to accommodate thousands more troops that were stationed there, new units that were activated and trained there, and units that were staged there from many other army posts until ordered to move to other locations.

World War II was the most important use period in Fort Hancock's history. Ironically this war's weapons and tactics made all American harbor defense forts obsolete, but just as ironically, the cold war era also gave Fort Hancock a second life when antiaircraft guns were deployed at the fort during the Korean War, which was quickly followed by the introduction of the Nike air defense missile system in 1954. This was the last defense system used at Fort Hancock from 1954 to 1974 when the Nike system and Fort Hancock were phased out. The story of Fort Hancock is so extensive that this book can only cover its first captivating era from the early years through the start of World War II.

One

FORTS BEFORE FORT HANCOCK

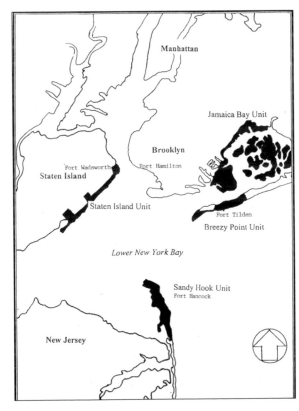

GATEWAY NATIONAL RECREATION AREA. Gateway National Recreation Area, created by an act of Congress in 1972, opened in 1974. The park preserves 26,000 acres of land and water around lower New York Harbor, including three of the four historic forts that once protected New York: Fort Hancock at Sandy Hook, Fort Tilden at Breezy Point, and Fort Wadsworth on Staten Island. (NPS.)

THE BRITISH INVADE NEW YORK CITY. During the summer of 1776, Gen. George Washington lacked the necessary manpower and heavy artillery to defend key locations around lower New York Harbor. This allowed a British fleet carrying 32,000 soldiers to sail unopposed by an undefended Sandy Hook into New York Harbor and fight the newly-formed American army in the Battle of Brooklyn on August 27, 1776. Though American forces won the revolution, the important lesson was learned that permanent forts were needed to defend harbors from attack by sea. This images is from *The Boys of '76. A History of the Battles of the Revolution* by Charles Carleton Coffin.

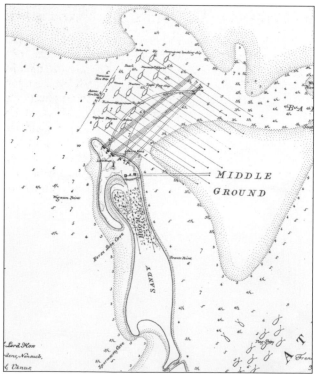

THE BRITISH DEFEND SANDY HOOK, JULY 1778. After the Battle of Monmouth on June 28, 1778, the British army evacuated Sandy Hook from July 1 to July 5. On July 7, a fleet of French warships anchored off the south end of Sandy Hook. Fearing the French would attempt to sail into the Sandy Hook channel and engage the British fleet, the British anchored their warships in three lines of battle to block the channel and quickly placed eight batteries of cannons from their fleet on Sandy Hook. The British defenses were so skillfully arranged that the French admiral, Comte Jean Baptiste Charles Henri Hector d'Estaing, pulled up his anchors and sailed away on July 22. (NA.)

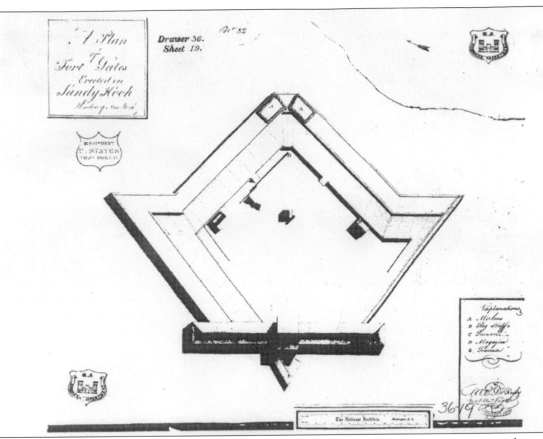

A PLAN OF FORT GATES, MAY 20, 1813. The first American harbor fortification constructed on Sandy Hook was Fort Gates, but it remains mysterious and elusive in the history of forts built there. It was likely named in honor of Revolutionary War general Horatio Gates, who died in 1806. It was known to be located somewhere north of Sandy Hook Lighthouse close to the tip of Sandy Hook where its cannons, probably a mix of 6, 12, 18, and 24 pounders, could effectively cover the Sandy Hook ship channel. The top center of the image shows the merlons (A), which are raised walls built atop the fort's parapet to create a vertical opening that a cannon could fire through while protecting the gun and gun crew. The flagstaff (B) was used for flying the national colors and perhaps also signaling flags. A hotshot furnace (C) was used by soldiers to heat up solid iron cannonballs until red hot to shoot them at enemy ships. Magazines (D) were structures used for storing gunpowder and cannonballs. The traverse (E) was a V-shaped defensive outwork placed outside a fort's outer wall. (SHU.)

FORT AT SANDY HOOK. Construction of an irregular pentagon-shaped, granite masonry fort with five bastions began in 1859. In this woodcut engraving from *Harper's Weekly* on December 8, 1860, construction is well under way with the fort's east (ocean) side wall on the left, and the north (harbor) side wall on the right, overlooking the tip end of Sandy Hook. The poles are steam-powered derrick cranes that lifted thousands of heavy, hand-cut granite blocks and other materials used in constructing the fort. Sandy Hook Lighthouse is seen in the left background. (AC.)

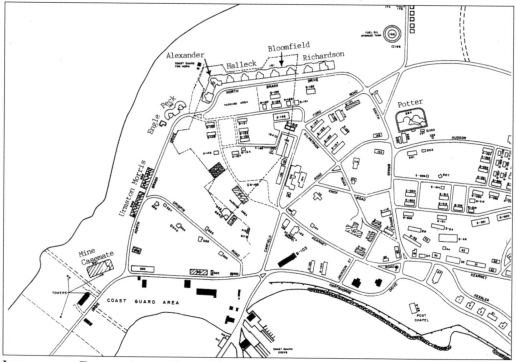

LOCATION OF FORT AT SANDY HOOK. This 1967 Fort Hancock Site Plan map shows fine dashed lines outlining where the Fort at Sandy Hook stood in relation to concrete gun batteries built between 1890 and 1910. (SHU.)

Two

NEW HARBOR DEFENSES

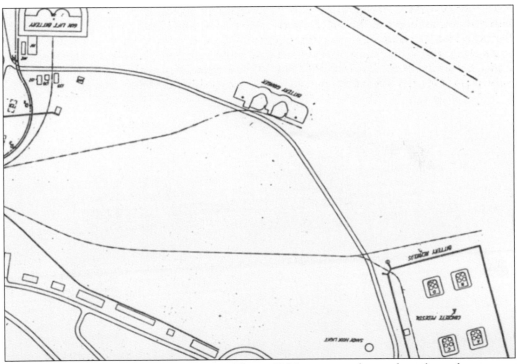

LOCATION OF THE FIRST GUN BATTERIES. This c. 1904 army map shows where the early concrete gun batteries were built in relation to the Sandy Hook Lighthouse. At upper left is the Gun Lift Battery (lift-gun battery number one), the first disappearing gun battery ever built in the United States. At lower right is Battery Reynolds, originally designated the Sandy Hook Mortar Battery. These two prototype batteries started the refortification of American harbors between 1890 and 1894. Between them is 10-Inch Gun Battery No. 1, later designated Battery Granger, built from 1896 to 1897. The lines seen going to these batteries were small gauge railroad spurs used first to bring in construction materials to these locations, then used to bring ammunition and equipment to them. (SHU.)

LIFT-GUN BATTERY NO. 1. America's first and only steam-powered disappearing gun battery is seen under construction during 1892. Cement mixing equipment was set up in the fall of 1890, and ground was broken in January 1891. Parts of the battery were built of granite taken from the Civil War-era "Fort at Sandy Hook," including this main entrance, which army engineers called a "defensible entrance to the battery." (SHU.)

MODEL 1892 BARBETTE CARRIAGE. This view shows a Model 1892 barbette carriage's configuration, including the loading platform that soldiers stood on to ram projectiles and powder bags into the breech of the gun. Two model 1891 barbette carriages were used on the steam-powered gun lift elevator platforms of Lift-Gun Battery No. 1. Since the lift guns were loaded by steam-powered ramrods, the loading platform seen here was not needed at the lift-gun battery. (MB.)

HOISTING UP THE FIRST GUN. By June 30, 1892, the north half of the lift-gun battery was completed, including the north lift-gun elevator mechanism. On August 29, 1892, a 12-inch breech-loading rifled gun, Model 1888, serial No. 11, weighing 52 tons and at a length of 36.5 feet, was hoisted to the top of the battery. It took 103 minutes to hoist the gun barrel to the top of the battery on a frame of large wooden timbers set up on the east side of the battery. (SHU.)

NORTH LIFT-GUN ON ITS CARRIAGE. Once the 12-inch gun barrel arrived on the roof of the battery on August 29, 1892, it was slowly moved via block and tackle on wooden logs, and placed on its model 1891 barbette carriage. With the 12-inch gun in position, Lift-Gun Battery No. 1 had the distinction of being the first Endicott System battery to be partially armed. The first trial of the entire mechanism, the lift-gun elevator, the ammunition hoist, and the hydraulic rammer, took place on August 31, 1892. (SHU.)

TEST FIRING THE NORTH LIFT-GUN. From September 12, 1892, to May 31, 1893, the north lift-gun was test fired a total of 24 times. This gave the battery the distinction of being the first Endicott System battery to be fired. The gun mechanism functioned with no problems during the tests, but the concrete of the parapet (the thick, wide, protective wall in front of the gun) was only four days old when firings began and had no time to harden before it was subjected to severe gun blasts. The result can be seen on the right. The parapet wall was rebuilt with a better type of concrete, raising the wall an extra 18 inches, and giving the concrete time to harden. (SHU.)

HOISTING THE SECOND GUN BARREL. By June 30, 1893, the masonry of the south half of the lift-gun battery was completed. Work on installing the south elevator mechanism continued that fall and winter until completed on February 8, 1894, but no carriage was available at the time. To conduct firing tests on the south elevator platform, the north elevator's carriage and gun was moved over to the south platform. It was not until May 17, 1895, that a second carriage was finally delivered for the south gun elevator platform, followed by a second 12-inch gun arriving on June 5, 1895, seen here being hoisted to the top of the battery. (SHU.)

THE SECOND 12-INCH GUN. On June 5, 1895, the second gun barrel, Model 1888, serial No. 12, arrived on top of the lift-gun battery and was mounted on the south elevator lift mechanism. On June 7, 1895, constructing engineer Col. George L. Gillespie, a Civil War Medal of Honor winner, notified the chief of army engineers that the battery was officially completed. Gillespie estimated that battery construction cost $455,028.23, and the armament and the assembling and mounting of it cost $141,458.93 for a total of $596,487.16. (APG.)

FRONT ENTRANCE, LIFT-GUN BATTERY NO. 1. This distinctive main entrance, seen here around 1894, is a unique architectural feature in the Endicott System of concrete gun batteries. Only at the lift-gun battery did army engineers build a traditional and architecturally unique main entrance from the Endicott era through World War II. Its main function was for defending the battery from attacking enemy infantry where soldiers could fire their rifles and three Gatling or Gardner machine guns through openings in the walls. On May 25, 1903, the battery was officially designated Battery Potter in honor of Brig. Gen. Joseph H. Potter, a Civil War veteran. (SHU.)

LIFT-GUNS ATOP BATTERY POTTER, C. 1899–1905. Battery Potter's range finding tower was built in 1899, so this photograph was probably taken during 1899–1905. The battery's design had several unique tactical features at the time for harbor defense. From atop the battery, these guns could fire at warships in all directions, including Sandy Hook's south end from which enemy forces might attack the hook's north end. (APG.)

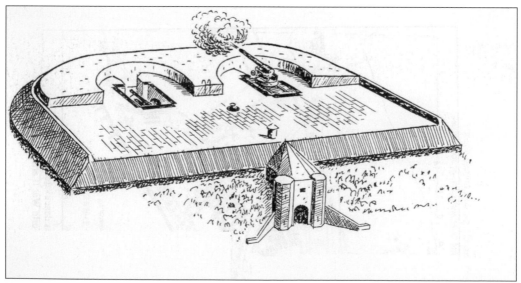

BATTERY POTTER IN ACTION. The battery's two guns were mounted on large elevator platforms powered by steam-driven hydraulic machinery. The guns were loaded inside the battery at the second floor level where they were protected and hidden from view by massive concrete walls. Here the left (north) gun is in loading position, and the right (south) gun is firing from the battery's roof. The guns could fire half-ton projectiles at approaching battleships and cruisers as far as seven miles offshore, but after firing they disappeared back down inside the battery for reloading. (SHU.)

CONSTRUCTING THE MORTAR BATTERY. Construction of America's first concrete mortar battery commenced in November 1890. Seen here on June 7, 1892, the battery's two front firing pits are side by side on the left, and the two rear firing pits are side by side on the right. The front and rear pits were connected by a 237-foot long main north-south tunnel and in the center of this tunnel is a cross east-west tunnel in which ammunition was stored. (SHU.)

COVERING THE MORTAR BATTERY. Thousands of tons of sand are piled around the battery's front firing pits, over most of the main tunnel, and most of the ammunition magazine tunnel. The west end of the magazine tunnel can still be seen sticking out of the hill of sand near the center of this February 8, 1893, photograph. Most of the sand slope earthworks covering the battery were completed by the spring of 1893. Due to the water table being close to the surface at Sandy Hook, the mortar battery was built at ground level and then covered or surrounded by sand slope earthworks, which gave them the deceiving appearance of being built underground when they were not. (SHU.)

AERIAL VIEW OF THE MORTAR BATTERY. This June 1919 aerial view shows the layout of the battery's four firing pits and the rectangular counterscarp wall enclosing them for defensive purposes. The lower and upper corners of the counterscarp wall had rooms built into them from which either Gatling or Gardner machine guns could fire down the open areas behind the walls to shoot down enemy infantry if they came over the walls. The historic first test firing of the battery took place on June 22, 1894. Five rounds were fired from the number one mortar in the northeast pit at a 45-degree elevation towards the ocean, and the Sandy Hook Mortar Battery became the first Endicott System mortar battery to be completed and its armament fired. (SHU.)

SANDY HOOK MORTAR PIT. Identified historically as the northwest firing pit, the upper left pit is seen in the above 1919 aerial view of the mortar battery. The mortar pits at Sandy Hook stood in pairs side by side, with pit A on the right and pit B on the left. In each firing pit, the mortar at the lower right is gun number one, the mortar at upper right is gun number two, the mortar at lower left is gun number three, and the mortar at upper left is gun number four. (SHU.)

SOLDIERS LOADING MORTARS. This *c.* 1910 photograph shows gun crews ramming half-ton projectiles into the breeches of the mortars. The four long poles with large sponge heads hanging on the pit walls were used to sponge out the mortars after firing to snuff out any smoldering gunpowder residue and to keep the bores clean. (SHU.)

READY TO FIRE. This view shows the pit and the mortars elevated and ready for firing. Soldiers stand behind each mortar holding lanyards, which were the cords pulled when the pit commander ordered them to fire. This ignited a primer set in the breechblock of each mortar, which ignited the powder charge inside the breech end of each mortar creating a massive explosion inside the mortars to shoot projectiles at targets. (APG.)

FIRING POSITION OF THE 12-INCH MORTAR. This is a rare view of a Model 1886 12-inch mortar mounted on a Model 1891 carriage. The wheels seen on each side at the top of the carriage were used to elevate the mortar from loading position to firing position. The hand cranks on the right and left sides of the carriage were used to traverse the circular gun platform to aim the mortar for firing in any direction. (APG.)

DETAIL OF BREECH, MODEL 1886 12-INCH MORTAR. The range of this model mortar was about 5.5 miles, sufficient enough to cover the immediate water areas around Sandy Hook in the 1890s and early 1900s. Only 84 of these model mortars and carriages were emplaced around the United States and in service from 1894 to 1920. (APG.)

LOADING 12-INCH MORTARS IN 1918. This photograph was taken in 1918 at Battery Seminole, Fort Taylor, Harbor Defenses of Key West, Florida. There are no known photographs of the mortars at Sandy Hook during World War I, but this provides an idea of what a mortar battery drill at Sandy Hook would have looked like. In this view, the mortar crews move quickly toward their mortars with their ammunition carts. (SHU.)

LOADING 12-INCH MORTARS IN 1918. This is another photograph taken in 1918 at Battery Seminole. The mortar crews get into position to ram projectiles into the front mortars while the rear ones have already been loaded. This view illustrates the crowded conditions in a mortar-firing pit, where four large mortars were serviced by up to 48 soldiers in each pit. (SHU.)

READYING THE 12-INCH MORTARS FOR FIRING. Here is a third photograph taken in 1918 at Battery Seminole, Fort Taylor, Harbor Defenses of Key West, Florida. Now loaded, the mortars are elevated for firing. Soldiers standing along the sides of the carriages man elevation wheels to bring the mortars up to their proper elevation, while other soldiers turn cranks to traverse the gun platforms to a set direction. The pit commander can be seen in the middle of the mortars. (SHU.)

FIRING ONE OF FOUR MORTARS. In this fourth photograph taken in 1918 a Battery Seminole, mortar number two has just fired, as indicated by the gun smoke. The soldier at lower right holds his lanyard, ready to fire mortar number three. In 1903, the Sandy Hook Mortar Battery was designated Battery Reynolds, in honor of Maj. Gen. John Reynolds, who was killed at the Battle of Gettysburg. In 1906, the battery was redesignated. The rear firing pits remained Battery Reynolds, but the front pits to the north were renamed Battery McCook, in honor of Civil War veteran Maj. Gen. Alexander McCook. (SHU.)

ANOTHER MORTAR IS FIRED. This photograph taken in 1918 at Battery Seminole shows gun smoke pouring out of mortar number one in the upper-middle as it fires off while the mortar crews stand at the lower-right waiting to move forward again to reload all four mortars. During practice drills, mortars were evidently fired individually or in pairs, but during a battle, all 16 mortars were fired at once. (SHU.)

THE MOMENT OF FIRING THE 12-INCH MORTAR. The tremendous explosive force of gunpowder coming out of the muzzle of a 12-inch mortar is caught by the camera in this view. Battery Anderson, Fort Monroe, Virginia, is pictured here. (SHU.)

MORTAR PIT TELEPHONE DATA BOOTH. In a mortar firing pit, mortar crews could not see what they were shooting at. They had to rely on other soldiers for spotting targets and directing their fire at moving targets. In 1905, data booths were placed in each firing pit at Sandy Hook to improve the communication of aiming instructions to mortar crews. Firing instructions were telephoned from soldiers spotting targets from a target spotting station built on top of Battery Potter to soldiers in the data booths. (SHU.)

A 12-INCH MORTAR ROUND HITS THE WATER. Seen here is the moment of impact when a half-ton 12-inch projectile hits the water during target practice. The object seen at far right is the brightly colored, sail-shaped target marker set on a floating sled being towed through the water by an army towing boat. Gun crews were not required to hit these targets because the small target represented a cruiser or battleship that was 400–600 feet long, so placing projectiles close to towed targets signified "hits" on an actual warship. (SHU.)

Three

FORT HANCOCK
TAKES SHAPE

FORT HANCOCK'S NAMESAKE.
On October 30, 1895, the war
department issued General
Order No. 57, which stated
that "the fortifications at Sandy
Hook, New Jersey, will hereafter
be known and designated as
Fort Hancock, in honor of the
late Maj. Gen. Winfield Scott
Hancock, United States Army."
A veteran of both the Mexican
and Civil Wars, he emerged
from the Civil War a national
hero, and because he was a
man of great integrity and high
ideals, he was nominated to be
a candidate for president of the
United States in 1880. (KBS.)

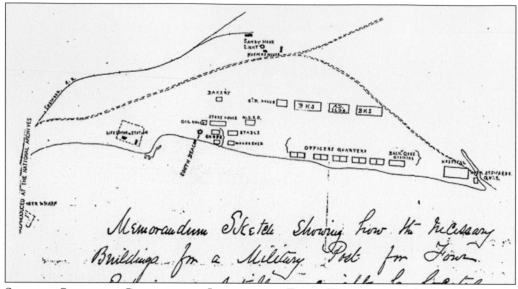

SKETCH SHOWING CONCEPTUAL LAYOUT OF FORT HANCOCK. Early in 1896, Maj. Gen. Thomas H. Ruger, commander of the department of the east, suggested to the war department that "barracks and other necessary buildings be erected as soon as possible" for a garrison of four batteries of heavy artillery be built to man Fort Hancock's new and additional gun batteries. Capt. Arthur Murray was chosen to prepare a conceptual plan. Murray reconnoitered Sandy Hook during the winter of 1896. The final layout of the post buildings as built in 1898 and 1899 were, for the most part, located as shown on Murray's rough sketch. (SHU.)

CAPT. ARTHUR MURRAY. Murray is shown as a cadet at the United States Military Academy in West Point, New York. Graduating second in his class in 1874, Murray was a captain commanding Battery L, 1st U.S. Artillery at Fort Wadsworth in 1896 when he was assigned to develop a master plan for a artillery post at Sandy Hook. Murray eventually attended the rank of general commanding the U.S. Army's Coast Artillery Corps. (WPA.)

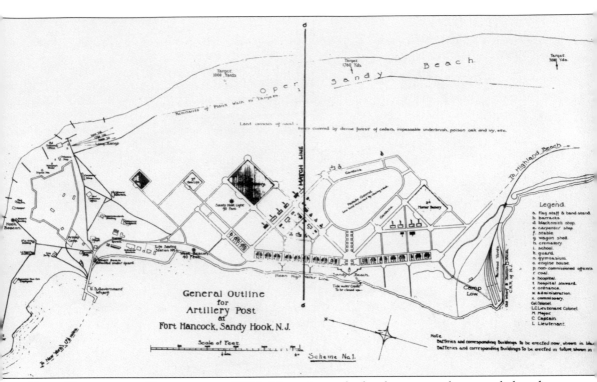

FORT HANCOCK AS PROPOSED, C. 1896. Murray's rough sketch was greatly expanded and refined by the U.S. Army Quartermaster Department's planning department, who drafted this detailed "General Outline for Artillery Post at Fort Hancock, Sandy Hook, N.J." This plan shows many more buildings than were actually built because Murray estimated that six batteries of artillerymen were needed for existing gun batteries, and that six more batteries of artillerymen would be needed to man additional gun batteries being planned for. (SHU.)

29

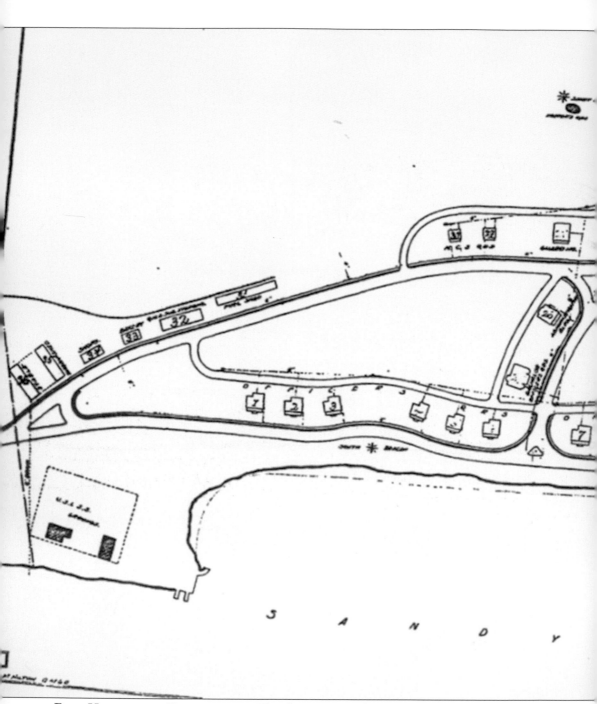

FORT HANCOCK AS BUILT, C. 1900 This fort site map shows 36 of the first 38 buildings built from 1897 to 1899, with north to the left on the map, south to the right, the east (ocean) side at

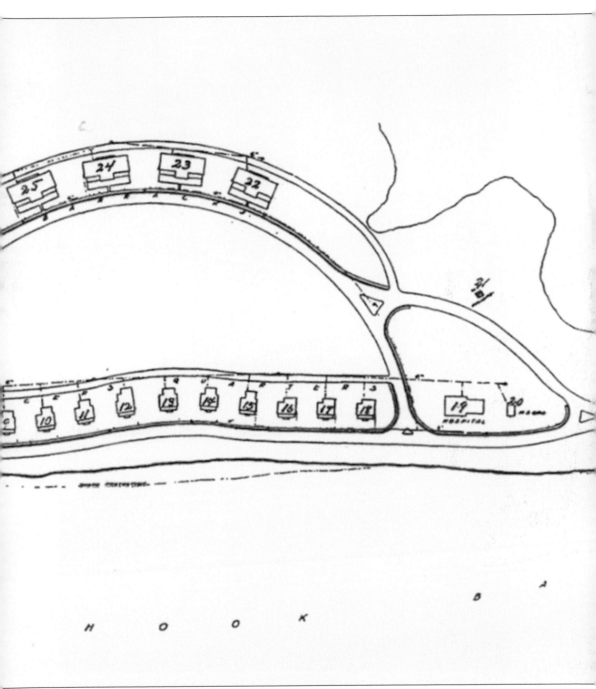

the top, and west (Sandy Hook Bay) at the bottom. (SHU.)

Capt. Carroll A. Devol. In late September 1896, Capt. Carroll A. Devol, seen here when he was quartermaster general later in his career, took over the Fort Hancock project as constructing quartermaster. Devol oversaw the many aspects of getting the fort built, including the letting out of construction bids on October 31, 1896, followed by executing contracts with contractors in December 1896. Devol planned to start construction work on March 1, 1897, and have it completed on or about October 31, 1897. Construction began in January 1897, but delays occurred. Devol was ordered to the Philippine Islands on May 24 and was replaced by Capt. George G. Bailey who oversaw the completion of the fort's buildings during 1898 and 1899. (SHU.)

VIEW OF FORT HANCOCK, N. J. LOOKING EAST.

OFFICER'S ROW. Perhaps the most outstanding architectural feature of Fort Hancock is its long line of officer's quarters known as Officers Row. Each of the 18 homes housed an officer and his family. Unlike other army posts, the fronts of these houses do not face the parade ground; they face Sandy Hook Bay where their spacious front porches could take full advantage of breathtaking sunsets. Also seen here is the West Beacon, a wooden lighthouse built in 1880 for bay side navigation as ships approached Sandy Hook from the west across Raritan and Sandy Hook Bays. (SHU.)

DETAIL VIEW OF FORT HANCOCK, C. 1902. This is one of the earliest views of Fort Hancock. Although undated, several structures in the photograph date this view to 1901 or 1902. It was taken from the roof of the Sandy Hook Proving Ground enlisted men's barracks, which was built in 1890. Note the roof and brick chimney of the building in the right foreground. (SHU.)

ORIGINAL FLAGSTAFF. On December 10, 1898, constructing quartermaster Capt. George G. Bailey recommended to the quartermaster general that a 100-foot iron flagstaff be erected on the north end of Fort Hancock's main parade ground. The flagstaff was at the post in January 1899, when Bailey advertised for bid proposals to construct a concrete foundation and erect the flagstaff. The low bidder was H. L. Brown, who was paid $550 for this work. In 1930, this flagstaff was replaced by another 100-foot flagpole that can still be seen. (SHU.)

FORT HANCOCK GARRISON ON REVIEW. This sweeping YMCA postcard view of the main parade, looking northwest, is titled "Regular Soldiers on parade, Fort Hancock, N.J." The fort was garrisoned by four companies of coast artillery (the 48th, 55th, 95th, and 113th Companies) from September 1903 to July 1907, which helps date the photograph. The buildings seen in the background, from right to left, are the post headquarters (building No. 26), bachelor officers' quarters (No. 27), Officers Row quarters (No. 5) which is partially hidden, then Officers Row quarters (Nos. 6 through 12). (SHU.)

OFFICERS ROW BUILDING NO. 1. Located at the north end of Officers Row, this house (seen around 1940–1941) was designated as building No. 1. The Army Quartermaster Department designed original architectural designs for both the 18 officers' quarters and four enlisted men's barracks. While all the officers' quarters exterior fronts looked the same, there were three officer grades on Officers Row. Houses 1–8 and 16–18 were designated "lieutenants' quarters." Each cost $8,290 and had the same interior floor plan with 4,552 square feet over three floors. (SHU.)

OFFICERS ROW BUILDING NO. 10, C. 1940–1941. Officers' quarters 9–11 and 13–15, were designated "captain's quarters." Their three upper floors totaled 4,750 square feet and there were five bedrooms on the second floor. Quarters No. 9 were completed on May 13, 1899, while quarters 10 through 15 were completed on September 19, 1899, each costing $13,694.80. (SHU.)

OFFICERS ROW BUILDING NO. 12. This photograph was taken by Thomas Smedley, a commercial photographer who was located on the Bowery in New York City and used to visit the post to take photographs from 1908 to 1916. Officers quarters No. 12 is seen with stripped, folded sun awnings on the front porch, ornamental hedges to the left and right of the front porch, three young shade trees, and two Civil War–era eight-inch Rodman guns on their carriages with two pyramidal piles of cannonballs as lawn ornaments. The guns were moved to Fort Monmouth in 1950. (SHU.)

OFFICERS ROW BUILDING NO. 12. The largest house on Officers Row was No. 12, the commanding officer's quarters. With the exception of houses 1–3, the rest of the Officers Row houses were completed in 1899, with quarters No. 12 completed on August 25, 1899. The interior floor plan differed from those of the lieutenants' and captain's quarters, as well as having the most rooms, totaling 5,402 square feet and costing $19,383.07 to build. (SHU.)

POST BUILDINGS FRONTING THE MAIN PARADE FIELD. This *c.* 1910–1912 panoramic view taken by Thomas Smedley shows some of the original post buildings built in 1898 and 1899. Fronting on the main parade field are, from left to right, bachelor officers' quarters No. 27, post headquarters No. 26, the roof of the YMCA building behind the trees, enlisted men's barracks 25, 24, 23, and 22, and "double company barracks 74." (SHU.)

FIRING A SALUTE. In this *c.* 1899–1901 view, soldiers fire a salute on the north parade field. In the background, from right to left, Officers Row quarters 1–4 can be seen, and just to the right of quarters 4 is the West Beacon. A wide space was left between quarters 4 and 5 so that no building lights would interfere with the West Beacon's light and that of the Sandy Hook Lighthouse for ships using them while navigating Sandy Hook Bay. (SHU.)

ENLISTED MEN'S BARRACKS BUILDING NO. 23. Like the officers' quarters buildings, the quartermaster department in Washington, D.C., designed this type of enlisted men's barracks especially for the Fort Hancock construction project. Located along the east side of the main parade field, the four barracks were aligned from north to south. Each cost $20,464.97, contained 14,762 square feet, and originally housed 70 soldiers including 60 enlisted men (privates), nine noncommissioned officers (corporals and sergeants), and one first sergeant. (SHU.)

COMPANY 136 POSES IN FRONT OF BARRACKS NO. 23. Fort Hancock changed from a four-company post to a six-company post when the 136th and 137th Mine Companies of Coast Artillery were organized on August 1, 1907. The 136th Company was formed by the transfer of four sergeants, five corporals, three specialists (a mechanic, musician, and cook), and 24 privates from another company. By April 30, 1912, when photographer Thomas Smedley took this photograph, Company 136th was apparently billeted in barracks No. 23. (SHU.)

EARLY VIEW OF BARRACKS ROW. This *c.* 1900 view was taken by William F. Oehler (1876–1971), a member of the 52nd Company of Coast Artillery. This view looking north shows barracks Nos. 23–25. Just beyond barracks No. 25 is building No. 28, the post guardhouse. (SHU.)

BARRACKS BUILDING NO. 24. This rare *c.* 1901 view looks north, showing barracks No. 24, the Sandy Hook Lighthouse, the southwest corner of the Mortar Battery's counterscarp wall, a new range-finding tower under construction, and the southwest corner earthwork slope of the Mortar Battery at far right. Note the soldiers' bedding being aired out over the back porch roof railings, and the two-wheeled cart in front of the back porch steps. (SHU.)

SOLDIERS ON "KP" (KITCHEN POLICE). Seven soldiers prepare a meal in barrack's building No. 25's kitchen around 1900. The first floor south wing of each enlisted man's barracks originally contained a kitchen room, pantry, cook's room, mess hall, and rooms for the company barber and tailor. "KP" was a much disliked duty, because soldiers "pulling" this duty had to get up extra early to report to the mess sergeant, put in a very long day of preparing three freshly made meals, and clean up before getting back into barracks that evening. (SHU.)

MESS HALL IN ENLISTED MEN'S BARRACKS. Since Pvt. William F. Oehler was billeted in barracks No. 25, this view is likely the mess hall in his barracks. The door in the left background leads into the hall where the barber and tailor shop rooms are located to the left, and the door on the right leads to the kitchen room. (SHU.)

TOM MIX, FIRST SERGEANT, AND HIS NON-COMMISSIONED OFFICERS, C. 1901–1902. On June 26, 1899, Battery O, 4th U.S. Artillery arrived at the Fort Hancock dock via the U.S. Army transport *General Meigs* from Fort Monroe, Virginia. This unit's first sergeant, Tom Mix, joined the army as a private during the Spanish-American War. He is seated front and center with his fellow non-commissioned officers (NCOs) on the front porch steps of barracks building No. 24. Mix left Fort Hancock on October 20, 1902, to become a famous cowboy movie star during the 1920s. (SHU.)

SOLDIERS POSING IN FRONT OF THEIR BARRACKS. The 48th Company is pictured here. The troops wear khaki colored uniforms, the result of the 1899 uniform regulations, which reflected changes made in army uniform policy following the Spanish-American War. Regular army units would now be issued drab-colored clothing, which was less conspicuous and made poorer targets in combat conditions compared to the traditional blue uniforms. (SHU.)

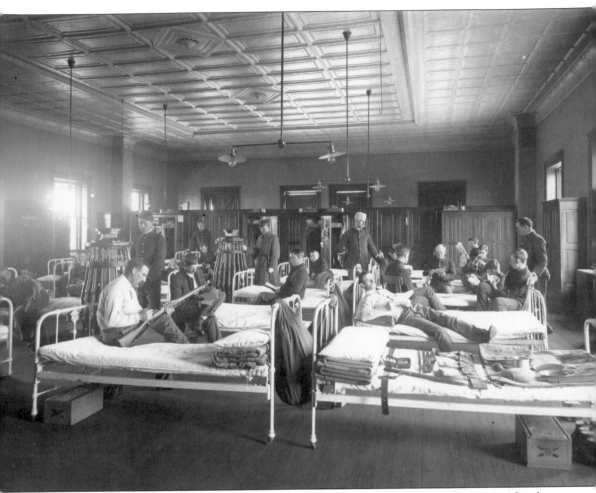

DETAIL VIEW INSIDE BARRACKS NO. 23, C. 1905. Although the soldiers are posing for the camera, they are doing typical things that soldiers did at permanent garrison posts. The soldier in the front left, sitting on his bunk is holding his 1903 Springfield rifle, which replaced the Krag-Jorgensen rifle around 1904–1905. Other soldiers lounge on their bunks while one, dressed in an overcoat, takes his rifle from the circular rifle rack. The footlocker at lower right is stenciled with crossed cannons and "55." Stationed at Fort Hancock as Battery I, 5th U.S. Artillery, the unit was redesignated as the 55th Company of Coast Artillery on February 18, 1901. The 55th Company served at Fort Hancock until February 17, 1909, when it transferred to Fort Mills in the Philippine Islands. (SHU.)

COMPANY 76 BASEBALL TEAM, C. 1912. Company 76 transferred from Fort Barrancas, Florida, to Fort Hancock on March 18, 1909, and occupied barracks No. 23. Shortly after arriving, Company 76 took part in the fort's annual service (target) practice, with the company manning and firing the eight 12-inch mortars of Battery McCook from June 7 to 22, 1909. These soldiers pose in front of the front porch of barracks No. 23 wearing baseball uniform shirts with "76 CO" on them. (SHU.)

A FORT HANCOCK FOOTBALL TEAM. Although team sports were a big part of army garrison life during the early 1900s, there is very little recorded information about the fort's athletic teams save for old photographs of them. Here a Fort Hancock football team poses along the south side of the post's gymnasium building No. 70. Since this building was built in 1909, this undated photograph was probably taken between 1910 and 1913. (SHU.)

MR. KAY'S GROCERY STORE. The 75th anniversary Fort Hancock souvenir booklet, issued by the U.S. Army in 1970, includes a similar photograph of this grocery store with the historic caption: "Kay's grocery store, the only civilian store on Sandy Hook. All groceries, produce, and meats were received two or three times a week from New York by government boat." (SHU.)

INSIDE MR. KAY'S GROCERY STORE. The clerks behind the counter, the lady, and little girl are not identified, but the counter and shelves of this grocery store are well stocked. (SHU.)

POST HEADQUARTERS BUILDING NO. 26. Also known as the "administration building" the post headquarters building was completed on July 25, 1899. Here the post commander, usually a colonel or lieutenant colonel, commanded the fort with a small administrative and officer staff. (SHU.)

BACHELOR OFFICERS QUARTERS BUILDING NO. 27. Located just to the west of the post headquarters, this building, seen here around 1940–1941, was completed on October 3, 1898. For many years the fort's officer's club was located in the front left (west) side room on the first floor adjoining the officer's dining room. (SHU.)

The Guard House, Sandy Hook, Fort Hancock, N. J. *Best wishes from Mary*

GUARDHOUSE BUILDING NO. 28. Completed on June 8, 1899, and costing $9,623.30, cells were designed for a capacity of 12 prisoners. The guardhouse served just like any town's police station, and here, every day of the year, a sergeant of the guard, a corporal of the guard, and 12 privates were posted for 24 hours of guard duty. Any soldiers who broke the army's rules and regulations could end up in the guardhouse, but sometimes even civilians ended up here. (SHU.)

SOLDIERS ON GUARD DUTY. Soldiers pose on the front porch of the guardhouse around 1903–1905. Some of the soldiers standing on the left appear to have the number 113 on their crossed-cannon hat insignia. The 113th Company coast artillery arrived at the fort on September 13, 1903, after being transferred from Fort McKinley, Maine. (SHU.)

POST HOSPITAL BUILDING NO. 19. Fort Hancock's construction project called for 32 buildings. While these were being built from 1897 to 1899, the surgeon general submitted plans to build a hospital building with a 12-bed south wing and quarters for a chief hospital steward. Construction began in 1897, and the hospital was completed on January 28, 1899, at a cost of $55,029.50. In 1902, a 12-bed addition was built onto the north side of the main hospital structure. In 1961, this building became a National Oceanic and Atmospheric Administration (NOAA) Marine Laboratory, but tragically, it burned down in September 1985. (SHU.)

HOSPITAL STEWARD'S QUARTERS BUILDING NO. 20. This single-family dwelling was completed on January 28, 1899, and cost $3,933. The building was almost lost on December 19, 1913, when an overheated stovepipe caused a fire on the second floor while occupied by SFC Paul Compton and his family. Luckily the fire was extinguished quickly. During 1959 or 1960, the original exterior walls were covered with phony brick face. (SHU.)

FORT HANCOCK'S OLDEST BUILDING. During initial plans to build the fort, a topographical map was prepared in 1896. This map shows a building, designated a "magazine," located on the spot of the building pictured here. What a magazine was doing here in 1896 remains a mystery, but evidently this building was either rehabilitated or rebuilt during 1898 while the fort's new buildings were being constructed. Interestingly, the fort's commanding officer asked the constructing quartermaster on September 27, 1898, to accept new NCO quarters Nos. 29 and 30 as soon as possible because his quartermaster-sergeant was "anxious to move into his [new] quarters, because he is currently living in an old powder magazine, and his wife was in poor health." This building was incorporated into the post's building number plan, assigned No. 21, and was used for both NCO and civilian employee housing. Originally a red brick structure, several wooden additions were added over the years, and its red brick exterior was painted yellow to match all of the other post buildings. (SHU.)

NON-COMMISSIONED OFFICERS QUARTERS BUILDING NO. 30. Sergeants Row started with two brick duplexes, each originally designated "Double Set N.C.O. Quarters." Each was designed to house two married sergeants and their families, and both were built using the same design plan. Building No. 29 was completed September 19, 1899, and building No. 30 was completed October 3, 1898, each costing $4841.24. Seven other non-commissioned officers quarters were built on Sergeants Row between 1906 and 1910. (SHU.)

COAL SHED-GARAGE BUILDING NO. 31. Of Fort Hancock's first 38 buildings, the first to be completed were coal shed building No. 31 and wagon shed building No. 35. The coal shed measured 21-feet-2-inches-by-169-feet and stored coal that was used in all of the post's buildings to create steam heat. The coal and wagon sheds were completed during August 1897. Eventually the coal shed was converted into a 16-car garage, seen here around 1940. When Fort Hancock closed in 1974, the building was still standing but was in derelict condition. It was demolished in 1981. (SHU.)

QUARTERMASTER OFFICE AND STOREHOUSE BUILDING NO. 32. To store everything the garrison needed to function, this large storehouse was built during 1897–1898. It consisted of a basement, one floor, and a loft. When it was decided to expand the post from four to six companies in 1907, the storehouse was already crammed with clothing, furniture, crockery, and gear. During 1910, a second floor was added. This was the building in which the remains of the Halyburton detachment, who died at Sandy Hook in 1783 while pursuing deserters from their warship. the H.M.S. *Assistance*, were boxed for burial in April 1908 (see page 86). (SHU.)

POST BAKERY BUILDING NO. 33. An essential part of the garrison's daily diet was fresh-baked bread. Originally referred to as the "bake shop," it was competed on December 19, 1898, at a cost of $8,937.35. In 1908, the post quartermaster noted the "congested condition" of the bakery. Because the fort had been expanded from four to six companies and also had to feed other visiting coast artillery companies practice firing the fort's guns, the increase in troops taxed the fort's support facilities. An addition to the bakery was approved and was completed by late July 1913 at a cost of $4,743. (SHU.)

WORKSHOP BUILDING NO. 34. This was another of Fort Hancock's first 38 buildings that were built between 1897 and 1899. Completed on September 19, 1899, at a cost of $3,745, this is where carpenters, plumbers, tinsmiths, and eventually electricians worked. During the 1930s, it was used as a Work Projects Administration (WPA) office. During November 1942, it was converted into a firemen's dormitory. One of the two firehouses located on the post, building No. 51, can be seen just to the left of the building in this photograph from 1940 or 1941. (SHU.)

"THE CORRAL," POST STABLES, BUILDING NO. 36. The U.S. Army was run on mule and horsepower for many years. In this *c.* 1910 photograph by Thomas Smedley, two soldiers pose on army horses while a soldier on sentry duty stands between them. Behind the mounted soldier on the left a wooden sentry booth can be seen. The original stables were built during 1898 and completed on January 28, 1899, at a cost of $8,258.30. (SHU.)

POST STABLES-ENLISTED MESS, BUILDING NO. 36. When this picture was taken around 1941, the former stables had been converted into an enlisted men's barracks. The army stopped using mules at the post in 1938, and the stables were converted into a barracks in February 1941 at a cost of $9,213. The sentry booth is long gone, and the building's appearance has changed compared to its original appearance in the photograph above. (SHU.)

Four

THE POST EXPANDS

CONSTRUCTING NINE-GUN BATTERY. Construction of what became the nine-gun battery began on March 31, 1897, and was designated "10-inch gun battery No. 2." As can be seen here, the battery was built over the east (ocean) side wall of the old Civil War masonry fort, much of which was taken down and used as a rip-rap seawall to protect the new gun battery. Originally the battery was to mount three 10-inch disappearing guns on newly developed counterweight carriages, the protective front concrete wall of which can be seen in the center of the photograph. (SHU.)

BATTERY GRANGER IN LOADING POSITION. A second lift-gun battery was planned to be built where this gun battery was located. This is the famous "Buffington-Croizer" counterweight disappearing carriage, which made Battery Potter's steam-powered lift-guns obsolete. The 10-inch gun, Model 1888, is seen here being loaded while hiding behind its protective frontal wall, which was 20 feet thick. The soldier at the top of the ladder aims the gun using a telescope while the soldier at lower right cranked the carriage to move the gun left or right. (SHU.)

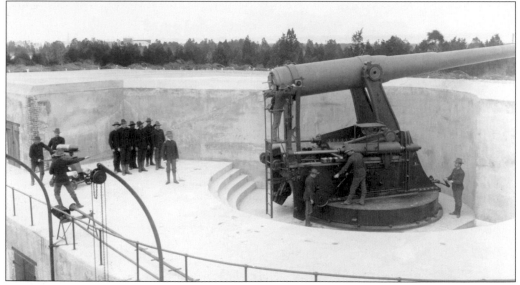

BATTERY GRANGER IN FIRING POSITION. Once the gun was loaded, one of the soldiers standing next to the carriage released a large counterweight, which was located under the gun. As the counterweight moved downward, it lifted the gun on large metal arms in just four or five seconds over the parapet into firing position, as seen here around 1899. Work on Fort Hancock's first counterweight disappearing gun battery started in June 1896, the masonry was completed in June 1897, and it was armed during 1897 and 1898, just in time for the Spanish-American War. (SHU.)

BATTERY GRANGER'S PARAPET. This is the top of the battery's parapet looking north toward New York Harbor. Counterweight gun batteries had thick, protective sand slopes piled to the top of the battery's frontal wall to protect them from enemy warships and also camouflage them from view. The only member of the gun crew who could see the target was the gun pointer looking out to sea in this photograph. In the left background, the lift-guns of Battery Potter can be seen, and to that battery's right, the Western Union Telegraph and Sandy Hook Proving Ground searchlight towers are also visible. (SHU.)

DISAPPEARING GUNS READY TO FIRE. In this c. 1899 companion view to the above photograph, Battery Granger's two 10-inch guns have raised up over the parapet into "in battery" (firing) position. The gun pointer is still standing at his observation post. When the guns were fired, the gun pointers had to remain at their post to continue to track targets out to sea. (SHU.)

BATTERY GRANGER'S ORIGINAL CONFIGURATION. On April 4, 1900, the war department officially designated 10-Inch Gun Battery No. 2 as Battery Granger in honor of Civil War veteran Maj. Gen. Gordon Granger. This is how the battery looked from around 1898 until a modernization project took place in 1907. Gun emplacement number one, on the right, is separated by the large, thick traverse wall in the middle from gun emplacement number two on the left. Behind each emplacement is a pair of davit cranes that soldiers used to hoist ammunition via block and tackle from the doorways. (SHU.)

BATTERY GRANGER AFTER ALTERATIONS. When Endicott-era gun batteries were first built, little was known about how to serve the guns quickly, adequate space to quickly service the guns, and how to accurately aim them to hit fast-moving targets. From 1899 onward, the army worked to improve these situations. In 1907, the gun emplacement platforms were extended and a battery commander's station (the concrete hut between the emplacements) was added so that the battery commander, usually a captain, could better command both guns from a central and protected position. (SHU.)

AMMUNITION CART AND TELEPHONE BOOTH. During modernization at disappearing gun batteries, new mechanical ammunition hoists systems were introduced. At Battery Granger, interior ammunition hoist shafts were installed. The soldiers seen here have rolled a projectile off the hoist onto an ammunition cart. For faster communication of gun aiming information, niches were installed so the soldier seen wearing earphones could give aiming instructions from target plotters to soldiers operating the gun. This view, along with the next four photographs, was taken at Battery Church, Fort Monroe, Virginia, between 1918 and 1925. (SHU.)

LOADING PROJECTILE INTO A 10-INCH DISAPPEARING GUN. Soldiers known as the ramming detail are seen here using their ramrod to push a projectile, weighing about 617 pounds, off its ammunition cart and into the breech of a 10-inch disappearing gun at Fort Monroe, Virginia, between 1918 and 1925. The ammunition hoist shafts at Battery Granger are located in the far left background. Behind the soldiers nearest the ammunition cart, a soldier is manning a large range board, two soldiers who open and close the breechblock stand at right, and above them the gun pointer tracks the target offshore. (SHU.)

SOLDIER AIMING A 10-INCH DISAPPEARING GUN. The 10-inch disappearing gun has been raised into firing position, and the gun pointer is tracking the target using a telescope while signaling the gun's elevation setter with his right hand to depress the gun. This is another view from Fort Monroe, Virginia, from around 1918–1925. Battery Granger at Fort Hancock strongly resembled this battery but one difference was that the gunners platforms were located on the right sides of Battery Granger's guns, while at Fort Monroe they are placed to the left. (SHU.)

LOADING A 10-INCH DISAPPEARING GUN. Under the watchful eye of an officer, the gun crew is ramming the projectile off its ammunition cart, and into the breech of a 10-inch gun at Fort Monroe, Virginia, between 1918 and 1925. At Fort Hancock, Battery Granger did not have the slanted type of stairs leading up to the parapet as seen here at Fort Monroe, but it had vertical, upright iron-rung ladders in the right corner of each emplacement. (SHU.)

READY TO FIRE THE 10-INCH DISAPPEARING GUN. Once loaded, the counterweight was dropped, bringing this 10-inch gun up over the parapet into firing position in four or five seconds. The simple design of this type of gun and emplacement allowed counterweight disappearing guns to be loaded and fired very quickly. A well-drilled gun crew could load and fire a 10- or 12-inch disappearing gun at a rate of two rounds per minute. At a typical two-gun disappearing gun battery, that worked out to be four rounds per minute. (SHU.)

DISAPPEARING GUN FIRING AT BATTERY GRANGER. The number one gun emplacement fires a round in this photograph from about 1935–1939. The gun seen here was 10-inch gun, Model 1888, mark II, serial No. 61, mounted on disappearing carriage, Model 1896, serial No. 19. In adjoining gun emplacement number two was 10-inch gun, Model 1888, serial No. 36, mounted on disappearing carriage, Model 1896, serial No. 20. Built of Rosendale cement and American Portland concrete, the battery was covered with waterproof paint, which was actually thick roofing tar. (SHU.)

BATTERY BLOOMFIELD BEING LOADED. When 10-Inch Gun Battery No. 2 was completed in 1898, the army continued to receive funding to build fortifications. What originally was planned to be a battery with three 10-inch guns now expanded into a seven-gun battery. The 12-Inch Gun Battery No. 2, built on the right (south) end of 10-Inch Gun Battery No. 2, is seen here being loaded around 1905–1906, just after it was named Battery Bloomfield in 1904, in honor of Revolutionary War general Joseph Bloomfield. The three 10-inch guns of 10-inch Gun Battery No. 2 were redesignated Battery Halleck, in honor of General Henry Halleck, a Civil War veteran. (SHU.)

BATTERY BLOOMFIELD READY TO FIRE. The 12-Inch Gun Battery No. 2 (Battery Bloomfield) was armed during October and Novembner 1889, with two 52-ton, Model 1888, MI½, 12-inch guns on Model 1896 disappearing carriages. The 12-Inch Gun Battery No. 3, built on the left (north) end of 10-Inch Gun Battery No. 2 (Battery Hallek) was armed in March 1900 with a pair of Model 1888 MII 12-inch guns on Model 1896 dissappearing carriages, and was named in honor of Revolutionary War general William Alexander in 1904. (SHU)

BATTERY RICHARDSON. With additional fortification funding, the army started building 12-Inch Gun Battery No. 4 onto the right (south) side of 12-Inch Gun Battery No. 2 in the fall of 1901. In 1904, a pair of Model 1900 guns were mounted on disappearing carriages. Fort Hancock now had a nine-gun battery, which could easily cover the Sandy Hook ship channel. Seen here is Battery Richardson's number one gun emplacement at the south end of the nine-gun battery around 1905. (SHU.)

EXPERIMENTAL LOADING RAMMER. In Battery Richardson's number two gun emplacement, an experimental ammunition loading mechanism was installed for field testing. This loading mechanism was mounted on a pair of semi-circular tracks installed in the concrete gun platform floor. Note the four powder bags behind the breech of the gun. The photograph was taken in 1904, when the Model 1900 guns were being mounted (note the gun on wooden blockage in the background). (SHU.)

FIRING POSITION OF THE 12-INCH DISAPPEARING GUN. By 1910, Battery Richardson's original Model 1900 12-inch guns had become badly eroded by repeated practice firings. These were replaced by a pair of Model 1895 M1 guns in March 1910. In this classic view from about 1940–1941, one of either Battery Bloomfield's or Battery Alexander's 12-inch disappearing guns, similar to those in adjacent Battery Richardson, is in firing position. Battery Richardson was named in honor of Brig. Gen. Israel B. Richardson, who was mortally wounded at the Battle of Antietam during the Civil War. (SHU.)

BATTERY RICHARDSON FIRES. The great explosive fire power of a 12-inch caliber, high-powered, disappearing gun firing is well demonstrated in this view from about 1905–1910 at Battery Richardson. The gun pointer's right arm is upraised as the gun goes off. Battery Richardson and adjoining Battery Bloomfield were used for annual service (target) practice for many years by both the Fort Hancock garrison and other New York Harbor fort units. (SHU.)

NINE-GUN BATTERY LOOKING NORTH. Taken from the south end of nine-gun battery looking north, the photograph was taken about 1921–1922 shortly after new concrete battery commander station huts were built at Batteries Richardson (seen here in the foreground), Bloomfield, and Alexander. The stations were completed in early April 1921 and transferred from the district army engineer to the coast artillery on June 27th.

NINE-GUN BATTERY, C. 1936-1939. This late 1930s view was taken at ground level from the south end of the battery looking north by John Bishop of the 52nd Coast Artillery. All of Fort Hancock's gun batteries are built at ground level and not underground as is often stated by people when they see or talk about the "bunkers" on Sandy Hook. The batteries simply could not be built underground because Sandy Hook is surrounded by water, which makes the water table only several feet under Sandy Hook's surface in most locations.

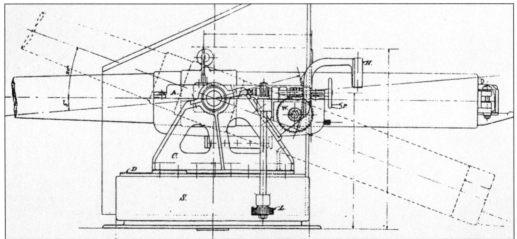

4.7" R.F. Gun mounted; pedestal mount with shield; concrete platform, sand protection; no magazine.
(Temporary concrete emplacement)

West end of the
Nine-Gun Battery
(Battery Alexander)

Emplacement for two 6" R.F. Guns on pedestal mounts, model 1900; concrete platform; ready for guns and mounts.
(Battery Peck)

One 5" R.F. Gun mounted; Balanced Pillar mount; concrete platform; serviceable.
(Battery Engle)

Northwest Bastion of Civil War Era "Fort at Sandy Hook."

RAPID FIRE GUN BATTERY LOCATIONS. During the Spanish-American War, an emergency battery was built in the sand dunes. This emplacement consisted of a "4.7-inch rapid fire gun mounted, pedestal mount with shield, [standing on a] concreted platform, [with] sand protection, no magazine." This temporary emplacement was joined by Battery Engle and Battery Peck. At middle and lower right is the north wall of the Civil War–era "Fort at Sandy Hook." (MB.)

THE 4.7-INCH SCHNEIDER GUN AND MOUNT. This is a cut-a-way side view drawing of a 4.7-inch Schneider gun and mount, the type of which was temporally emplaced at Sandy Hook during the Spanish-American War. A number of different 4.7-inch guns were purchased by the U.S. Army Ordnance Department for testing during the mid-1890s. This was the only 4.7-inch Schneider gun emplacement that was used for American coastal defense. In 1904, it was removed by Sandy Hook Proving Ground personnel. (MB.)

BATTERY ENGLE. Construction of this one-gun battery started on September 5, 1897, and finished on April 21, 1898, just four days before Congress declared war on Spain. Mounted in the emplacement was a five-inch breech-loading rapid-fire gun, Model 1897, serial No. 2, mounted on a balanced pillar carriage, Model 1896, serial No. 2. The battery was named in honor of Capt. Archibald H. Engle who was killed in the Civil War. There is no known photograph of Battery Engle, but it looked like Battery Vicars, Fort Worden, pictured here. (MB.)

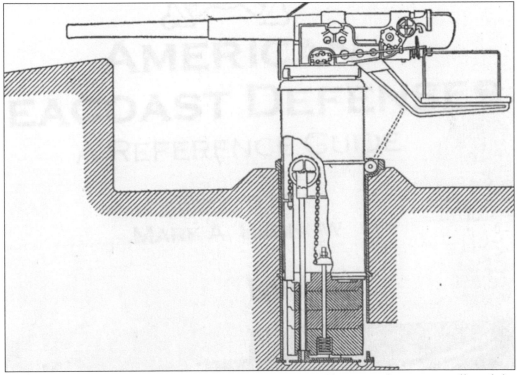

DRAWING OF A MODEL 1896 BALANCED PILLAR MOUNT. This type of gun mount allowed the gun to come up over the protective parapet wall of an emplacement to fire. When not in use, the gun could be turned sideways in the emplacement with the muzzle end of the gun barrel in a niche located in the side of the emplacement. Battery Engle ended up being located on the left flank of Battery Peck when that gun battery was built in 1903. Battery Engle was declared obsolete and disarmed in 1918. (MB.)

BATTERY PECK, C. 1905–1910. This battery was constructed between 1901 and 1902 and armed with two guns mounted on barbette carriages in September 1903. Battery Peck was part of the army's underwater mine defense in lower New York Harbor, where it would defend against fast, shallow-draft warships like torpedo boats, destroyers, mine-sweepers, and enemy landing craft. It was named in 1903 after Lt. Fremont P. Peck who was mortally wounded by a bursting gun at the Sandy Hook Proving Ground on February 19, 1895. (AC.)

BATTERY PECK'S GUN EMPLACEMENT NUMBER ONE. Seen here between 1910 and 1930 is the east side gun, with the west end earthwork slope of the nine-gun battery seen behind the gun. The two buildings to the left housed the foghorn at Sandy Hook. This was a Model 1900 gun, serial No. 27, mounted on Model 1900 barbette carriage, serial No. 12. Note the protective canvas covers over the breech and the curved elevation drum mechanism. Today the area seen behind the gun is heavily overgrown with vegetation. (SHU.)

BATTERY PECK'S GUN EMPLACEMENT NUMBER TWO. This is the west side six-inch gun, Model 1900, serial No. 28, mounted on a Model 1900 barbette carriage, serial No. 17. Behind the back part of the gun is the battery's coincidence horizontal-base range finder (CFR) station that was built over the gun emplacement of former Battery Engle in 1920. The Model 1900 barbette mounted six-inch gun had an effective range of well over 10 miles. (SHU.)

BATTERY PECK'S BATTERY COMMANDER STATION. The battery commander's station was built into the earthwork traverse between the battery's two guns. Originally it was open to the sky. During 1920, an enclosed concrete battery commander's station was built and is seen here in 1921. An interesting item can be partially seen just to the left of the hut covered by a canvas tarp. This is a mobile mounted Model 1917 three-inch antiaircraft gun. (SHU.)

THREE-INCH RAPID FIRE GUN, MODEL 1902. Over 250 three-inch guns were installed in American harbor defenses between 1899 and 1917. Two three-inch rapid-fire gun batteries were built at Fort Hancock. Battery Urmston consisted of four Model 1898 guns on balanced pillar mounts that were installed in 1903, followed by two Model 1903 pedestal-mounted guns installed in 1909. Located just east of Urmston was Battery Morris, where four Model 1903 pedestal-mounted guns were emplaced in 1909. The Model 1903 guns and carriages strongly resembled the Model 1902 gun and carriage pictured here. (SCA.)

BATTERY MORRIS AND BATTERY URMSTON. This close-up view shows four soldiers manning a three-inch gun at Battery Irwin at Fort Monroe, Virginia, in 1918. The soldiers standing along side the gun are aiming, elevating, and traversing it. The soldier at left is holding the lanyard which, when pulled, will fire the gun. Batteries Morris and Urmston, which mounted three-inch guns that resembled this one, were assigned to the mine defense of the harbor, covering the "water area from the entrance to Ambrose Channel to a point west of Sandy Hook." (SHU.)

BATTERY MORRIS. This is a breech-end view of a Model 1903 three-inch rapid-fire gun at Battery Morris. The breechblock is in the open position, and three rounds have been lined up for the photograph. Rapid-fire three-inch guns fired fixed ammunition which allowed a three-inch gun to fire up to 15 rounds per minute. The six guns of Battery Urmston and the four guns of Battery Morris firing at once would send a lot of projectiles toward enemy warships every minute. In 1904, Battery Morris was named in honor of Col. Lewis Morris who was killed in the Civil War. (SHU.)

BATTERY MORRIS RANGE FINDING STATION. This "closed type" coincidence horizontal-base range finder (CFR) station was built just to the east of Battery Morris in 1920 to better aim the battery's four three-inch rapid-fire guns. The battery had a long service life from 1909 to 1946 when it was declared obsolete and scraped. Today the battery's range-finding station is hardly visible due to heavy undergrowth all around it, which is a far cry from when this photograph was taken around 1921. (SHU.)

BATTERY URMSTON. Two of the battery's six three-inch rapid-fire guns are seen here ready to be fired between 1904 and 1908. Note the officer standing on the traverse between gun emplacements numbers one (right) and two (left). At this time, the battery did not have an enclosed battery commander station, and the officer had to stand out in the open. A combined battery commander's station and coincidence horizontal-base range finder (CRF) station was not built until 1918. In 1904, Battery Urmston was named in honor of Lt. Thomas D. Urmston who was killed in the Civil War. (SHU.)

BATTERY URMSTON. This view shows soldiers waiting to bring up fixed ammunition to the gunners manning gun emplacements. These are two of the four masking parapet balance-pillar mounts at the battery, which could be raised up over the protective parapet wall when in use and then down and sideways with the guns muzzles fitting into small niches in each emplacement when not in use. These mounts never did good service in the Coast Artillery Corps, and the ones at Urmston were dismounted and removed in 1920. (SHU.)

BATTERY GUNNISON'S NORTH EMPLACEMENT. Rounding out Fort Hancock's rapid fire gun batteries was Battery Gunnison. Originally the army wanted to build this battery in 1898 in the sand dunes southeast of the south end of the nine-gun battery but this was proving ground property. A site was finally chosen, and the battery was built in 1904. This photograph, taken between 1933 and 1936, shows the north number two emplacement of the battery, which mounted a Model 1903 gun and Model 1903 disappearing carriage that was emplaced on March 14, 1908. A similar model gun and carriage were emplaced in gun emplacement number one on February 12, 1906. (SHU.)

BATTERY GUNNISON. This photograph, taken between 1933 and 1936, shows the breech-end view of gun emplacement number two. A couple of soldiers are up on the gun pointers platforms which flank the gun. During 1943, this gun and carriage and the adjoining gun and carriage were removed. Each emplacement was filled with new concrete almost to the top of the protective parapet wall seen here. Battery Peck's two six-inch barbette mounted guns were then brought to this battery and installed on the new gun platforms. (SHU.)

71

BATTERY GUNNISON'S TRAVERSE AND BATTERY COMMANDER'S STATION. The door on the right is the battery's storeroom, and the doors in the wall between the staircase leading up to the concrete and wooden battery commander's station hut go into the battery's plotting room, where ranges were plotted for the gunners manning the battery's guns. Also inside this traverse were the magazine rooms, one for storing 600 six-inch projectiles and the other for storing 600 powder charges. (SHU.)

BATTERY GUNNISON'S SOUTH EMPLACEMENT. This photograph, taken c. 1933–1936, shows gun emplacement number one in a six-inch disappearing gun battery that is very similar in construction to Battey Gunnison. The gun crew is ramming in a projectile. Although the battery had ammunition carts, those young, strong soldiers could carry the 105- and 108-pound projectiles from the magazines right up to the breech of the gun where the projectile was rammed in first, followed by a powder bag. The gun pointer is up on the gunner's platform zeroing in on a target while the rest of the gun crew loads and traverses the gun. (SHU.)

BATTERY GUNNISON'S SOUTH EMPLACEMENT. This view from 1940 or 1941 is looking from the south number one gun emplacement toward the battery's traverse and battery commander's station. The soldier at the flag pole is running up a red flag, which is the signal to all boats and ships in the area that live target practice is about to begin. Wearing blue denim work fatigues, soldiers stand by the breech of the gun and by railings waiting for word to start the drill. (SHU.)

OBSERVING A TARGET AT BATTERY GUNNISON. This sharp-looking army officer is peering though a high-powered spotting scope to zero in on the target offshore around 1940–1941. While most of the battery commander stations at Fort Hancock were made of concrete, the one seen here at Gunnison had front and side walls made of concrete but a rear wall and roof made of wood. Battery Gunnison was named in 1904 in honor of Capt. John W. Gunnison, who was killed by Native Americans in Utah Territory in 1853. (SHU.)

SOUTHWEST CIVIL WAR FORT BASTION. Fort Hancock's mine casemate was originally located inside the southwest bastion during the Civil War. Inside this bastion were two large rooms: one to detonate underwater mines and one where insulated cables went down into an underground cable run tunnel. From here, the cables ran underwater around the tip of Sandy Hook and out to distributions boxes on the floor of the harbor where other insulated electric cables ran out to each individual mine. This view was taken before 1910. (SHU.)

UNDERWATER MINE DEFENSES IN 1898. This map shows the controlled mine fields stretching across the entrance to lower New York Harbor. The army planted mines in groups with each mine and mine group numbered. Mines could be detonated individually or in groups. The mines were planted in shallow water areas to destroy fast moving, shallow-draft warships from below, while rapid-fire gun batteries fired at them on the surface. (SHU.)

CONTROLLED UNDERWATER MINE. Mine casings were buoyant and attached to an anchor to keep it in a precise location. An electrical cable came out of the distribution box so that the mine could be exploded from the mine casemate on Sandy Hook. All the numbered mines were marked on a detailed harbor map so their exact positions were known to observers at the mine casemate. Headquarters Battery and Batteries A, B, and D, 7th Coast Artillery Regiment, manned the mine defenses at different times during 1924 to 1941 at Fort Hancock. (SCA.)

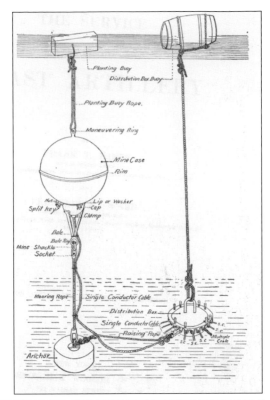

A U.S ARMY MINE PLANTER. The army operated boats officially called mine planters that placed controlled mines in harbors. For many years the mine planter *General E. O. C. Ord* (MPB-6) was stationed at Fort Hancock and served from 1909 to 1946. Seen here is the mine planter *General Samuel M. Mills*, which served elsewhere in the Coast Artillery Corps. A mine anchor (left) and buoyant mine (right) can be seen hanging over the side of the boat. This photograph was taken around 1910–1915. (AC.)

SEARCHLIGHT IN ITS SHELTER. Another important component of the harbor defenses were searchlights. In case of night attacks, the Coast Artillery Corps used searchlights to locate and illuminate enemy warships. Fort Hancock received its first searchlights, a 36- and a 60-inch, in 1904. A site for the 60-inch light was selected 250 yards south of Battery Gunnison, where a dome-shaped sand embankment hill was formed to position the light in a wooden shelter. (SHU.)

SEARCHLIGHT OUT SIDE ITS SHELTER. The 60-inch searchlight located south of Battery Gunnison was mounted on tracks so the light could be rolled out of its shelter for use, then back in to not only shelter it from the weather, but also to hide it from view. A concrete generator building was erected opposite the searchlight in 1904 and can still be seen today on Atlantic Drive. (SHU.)

DISAPPEARING SEARCHLIGHT TOWER IN DOWN POSITION. During 1917, two ingenious disappearing searchlight towers were constructed at Sandy Hook. Since both were experimental, they were located close to each other in a wooded, back dune area, over a mile south of Battery Gunnison. One tower, designated type C design, was the work of army assistant engineer E. D. Cummings, while the other was designed by the Strauss Bascule Bridge Company of Chicago. (SHU.)

DISAPPEARING SEARCHLIGHT TOWER IN UP POSITION. Each steel-girder tower had a concrete counterweight, which lifted the tower up. As the tower moved up, the searchlight platform pivoted on its platform so the light stayed upright when the tower stood up. After testing during 1917 and 1918, the towers and a generator building were transferred to the Coast Artillery in August 1918. These interesting and unique searchlight towers remained in service through World War II. (SHU.)

DISARMING BATTERY POTTER. By 1905, Fort Hancock had 11 gun batteries in service besides Battery Potter. Battery Potter was made technically obsolete when counterweight carriages were introduced in 1894. The one thing that saved it from scrapping was the fact that its two guns could fire in all directions while the newer counterweight disappearing gun batteries could not. However the army finally decided to dismantle the battery guns and carriages, as seen in this 1906 view. (SHU.)

DISMANTLED GUNS ATOP BATTERY POTTER. This August 1906 rooftop view shows two soldiers sitting on the semicircular concrete steps that lead from the battery's terreplein (roof) in the foreground up onto the protective concrete parapet that once shielded the guns. The gun barrels and barbette carriages that once mounted the guns can be seen lying on top of the parapet. Battery Potter's machinery was eventually removed as scrap during 1909 and 1910. (SHU.)

PRIMARY FIRE CONTROL STATIONS ATOP BATTERY POTTER. During 1907, Battery Potter was converted into the primary fire control center for directing the artillery fire of all Fort Hancock's gun batteries. The conversion actually started in 1905, when the wooden fire control observation and plotting room station building seen on the roof at right was built. This observation station controlled the fire of mortar Batteries McCook and Reynolds at targets offshore. The long concrete and wooden building (left) housed observation and plotting room stations for, from right to left, Batteries Gunnison, Granger, Richardson, Bloomfield, Halleck, Alexander, and Peck. (SHU.)

FIRE CONTROL AND TELEPHONE COMMUNICATION BUILDINGS AT BATTERY POTTER. This view from about 1907 shows the wooden fire control building atop Battery Potter, built in 1905, for directing the artillery fire of mortar Batteries McCook and Reynolds. The two concrete buildings build at ground level were telephone switchboard communications buildings built in 1907. Here army personnel connected the target plotters atop Potter to the fort's gun batteries via telephone to relay range information directly to the gun crews. (SHU.)

TARGET PLOTTING ROOM ATOP BATTERY POTTER. This is one of the two plotting rooms in the wooden fire control station building built on top of Battery Potter in 1905. These soldiers are receiving range data from spotters using high-powered telescopes on the upper floor of the station and are plotting the range, speed, and direction of a target offshore on the semicircular fire commander's plotting board seen here. (SHU.)

BATTERY ARROWSMITH. When Battery Potter was dismantled in 1906, the army lost a gun battery that had provided long-range artillery fire in all directions around Sandy Hook. To cover the bay side, Battery Arrowsmith was constructed on the point of Horseshoe Cove during 1907–1908, and armed during December 1909, with three eight-inch Model 1888 guns. (MB.)

**BATTERY ARROWSMITH'S
NAMESAKE.** George Arrowsmith
was born in 1839. When the Civil
War erupted, Arrowsmith joined a
New York regiment of volunteers.
He eventually became lieutenant
colonel of the 157th New York
Volunteer Regiment, which he
was gallantly leading into battle
at Gettysburg when he was killed
on July 1, 1863. When GAR
Arrowsmith Post No. 61 heard
that the army was building a new
gun battery at Fort Hancock, the
membership asked the secretary
of war to name it after George
Arrowsmith, which was done
on June 17, 1908. This forgotten
hero quietly lies in his family's
burial plot at Fairview Cemetery
in Middletown Township. This
photograph is from *The New Jersey
Coast in Three Centuries*, Vol. 1, by
editor William Nelson.

**JOHN J. MULHERN AT BATTERY
ARROWSMITH.** John J. Mulhern's
father, Francis, brought his wife,
Anna, and children John and Mary to
Fort Hancock during the summer of
1908 when he took the job of fireman
at the post's water pumping station.
John was just four years old when the
family arrived, and he would grow
up and be part of Fort Hancock's
formative years from 1908 to 1927.
He attended Rutgers University from
1924 to 1927, and during this time he
was a cadet in the army ROTC. Here
he poses with the covered breech of
one of the eight-inch disappearing
guns at Battery Arrowsmith around
1926–1927. (SHU.)

COMMISSARY BUILDING NO. 47. Rations were issued from commissary warehouses which were referred to as commissaries. Albin Zwiazek of the 52nd Coast Artillery remembers, "The commissary was where officers and N.C.O.'s and their wives could buy food items. Say if an N.C.O.'s wife didn't buy coffee at a local store in one of the towns near Sandy Hook, she could buy it at the commissary, where it was cheaper in price compared to local stores. Also, some of the sergeants who lived off the post in local towns would carry out their groceries from the commissary in brown paper bags to their cars, so we [soldiers] used to jokingly call those sergeants the 'brown bag brigade.'" (SHU.)

POST EXCHANGE BUILDING NO. 53. Fort Hancock's first post exchange building was a wood frame building that was heavily damaged in a 1901 fire and, while repairs were made, a new and larger building was needed. Construction began in July 1904, behind and east of the YMCA building and was completed in July 1905 at a cost of about $10,000. By 1909, with six companies posted at Fort Hancock, the post exchange needed to be expanded. The addition was completed in March 1910 and cost $14,800. (SHU.)

MESS HALL BUILDING NO. 57, C. 1940–1941. During 1900, the army knew that if the Fort Hancock garrison was ever expanded, the post would need more barracks space. One of the alternatives considered was to create more bunk space in barracks Nos. 22–25, but to do so, each barracks kitchen and mess hall would have to be converted into dormitory space. As a result, four "detached kitchen/mess hall" buildings were completed, inspected, and accepted by the post commander in mid-June, 1905. (SHU.)

SOLDIERS AT MESS. Seen here is a rare 1905 or 1906 view of Fort Hancock soldiers in one of the four detached mess halls built in 1905. Mess hall building No. 55 was located behind barracks No. 22, mess hall building No. 56 was located behind barracks No. 23, mess hall building No. 57 was located behind barracks No. 24, and mess hall building No. 58 was located behind barracks No. 25. In each barracks, the former mess halls and kitchens were converted into additional dormitory space. (APG.)

SOLDIERS ON "KP" DUTY. No one is identified in this group of somber looking soldiers, but photographer Thomas Smedley captured these fellows while on kitchen police duty on the porch steps located on the east side of barracks No. 74 in October 1911. The soldiers are holding a variety of kitchen utensils including a saw and butcher knife at left. (SHU.)

ENJOYING THANKSGIVING DINNER. It is Thanksgiving Day in 1911, and five young soldiers of the 113th Company have invited two young ladies to enjoy dinner in the pantry room of one of the four mess hall buildings built in 1905. A close look at the table reveals a cooked turkey and a bowl full of gravy at lower left. To the right of this bowl is a box of Royal Scarlet cigars. Two bowls holding celery stalks and two plates full of apples can be seen, along with two bowls of olives, a platter of sweet potatoes, and as a centerpiece, large pinecones in a dish. (SHU.)

SGT. MAX DUZE. Max Duze's son Bernie recalled: "Dad came from Russia or Poland all by himself as a teenager and joined the U.S. Army. When he was older, all the younger soldiers thought that he had never left the post and seen any action. Well, my dad never talked about it to anyone, but during a German night attack in WWI he heard a fellow soldier yelling for help. He put the wounded soldier over his shoulder and ran for cover across the muddy ground in his stock feet. Mind you, IN HIS STOCKING FEET! For saving this soldier, dad was awarded the Silver Star for gallantry in action." (SHU.)

THE DUZE FAMILY QUARTERS. The senior-most sergeants lived on Sergeants Row, but the lesser-grade married sergeants had to live in smaller wooden buildings scattered around the post. John J. Mulhern recalled: "Whenever a junior grade sergeant arrived he either bought the house from the sergeant who was transferring, or, if no house was available, he would go to the post commander to ask permission to build a small house. Some of the sergeants actually built some of the homes from prefabricated kits you could buy from Sears Roebuck and Montgomery Ward back then." Seen here is Max Duze's house that stood on Magruder Road. (SHU.)

DISCOVERY OF THE HALYBURTON BURIAL VAULT. On December 31, 1783, Hamilton Douglas Halyburton and 13 others died tragically in a blizzard at Sandy Hook while pursuing deserters from their warship, the H.M.S. *Assistance*. Their burial vault lay lost and forgotten until April 15, 1908, when it was accidentally discovered by laborers excavating a roadbed near Horseshoe Cove. Here the labor crew poses with the remains. Look closely to the left of the skull and a pair of shoes can be seen still on the feet. (SHU.)

PVT. LANDER W. RADFORD. Pvt. Lander W. Radford was on duty in building No. 32 in April 1908 when workmen arrived with the remains of Lt. Hamilton Douglas Halyburton and his comrades who had died at Sandy Hook in 1783. Radford recalled that "We were told that 14 bodies were found in a forgotten burial vault, so we were ordered to make 14 wooden boxes to hold each body. But the trouble was that all the bones were mixed together in the boxes brought to the storehouse. We couldn't tell who was who, so when we made the boxes we did our best to try and figure out if we had enough bones for each body, and then put them into each box." (SHU.)

BUGLER THOMAS SHEEHAN. Thomas Sheehan served in the 113th Company. Since his company was stationed at Fort Hancock from September 1903 to July 1916, this photograph was taken during that time. John J. Mulhern recalled: "Back in the old U.S. Army they used to say 'You can set your watch by the bugle calls,' and that was very true. From '1st call' and 'reveille' early in the morning, then different calls throughout the day, to 'lights out' and 'taps,' each call was blown at a precise time, so you could be anywhere on the post, and you knew what time it was, and you knew what was going on as well." (SHU.)

MEDICAL STAFF POSING AT THE POST HOSPITAL. This posed view was taken in June 1915 on the front porch of the post hospital building No. 19. Only one soldier, Harry Fitzpatrick, is identified, sitting in the first row at far left. Like all of the army's branches, the Coast Artillery Corps would retain the traditional "army blues" uniform well into the 20th century. However, in June 1916, Gen. Leonard Wood, commander of the eastern department, contacted his post and regimental commanders to comment on the advisability of eliminating the enlisted men's blue uniform and make the olive drab uniform mandatory. The Fort Hancock commander agreed. (SHU.)

REAR OF THE POST HOSPITAL AND ANNEX. Old photographs of the post hospital usually show only the nice-looking front (west) side of the building. Here is a rare view taken by John Bishop of the 52nd Coast Artillery between 1936 and 1939, showing the rear (east) side of (from the right) the north wing and main middle section of the post hospital and the annex building. The main middle section was completed in 1899, the 12-bed north wing in 1902, and the annex in 1905. When the Sandy Hook Proving Ground was designated a permanent facility in 1901, the Fort Hancock hospital was expected to provide care for the proving ground ordnance detachment, as well as the fort's four companies of coast artillery. This justified building the annex in 1905. (SHU.)

POST MORGUE BUILDING NO. 54. Originally referred to as the "Deadhouse," this one-story, 20-by-32-foot building was built at the same time and of the same materials as the annex in 1905. The morgue was completed on February 27, 1905, at a cost of $2,863. The sign at the left corner of the building states "Recruiting Office U.S. Army." When the author showed this photograph to a reunion group of 7th, 52nd, and 245th Coast Artillery veterans back in the 1970s, there were howls of laughter over that sign. (SHU.)

FORT HANCOCK YMCA.
In 1901, William R. Millar, secretary of the YMCA, met with the secretary of war to inform him that the YMCA was willing to provide $15,000 for erecting a building at Fort Hancock. It would contain reading, recreation, and correspondence rooms, a gymnasium, and smaller rooms for meeting and Bible readings for the garrison, and its architectural style would be similar to the other Fort Hancock buildings. As seen here in a YMCA postcard dated September 25, 1905, it was built and its facilities opened to the soldiers during the winter of 1903–1904. (SHU.)

ARMY ASSOCIATION BUILDING, FORT HANCOCK

1ST M.E. CHURCH   REV.A.A.BROWN
FORT HANCOCK N.J.

FIRST METHODIST CHURCH. This postcard caption reads "1st M.E. Church, Rev. A.A Brown, Fort Hancock, N.J." The structure strongly resembles what was known as Saint Mary's Chapel, a Roman Catholic chapel. If these buildings were one and the same, the chapel building originally stood on the northeast corner at the intersection of Kearney and Canfield Roads. In 1904 or early 1905, it was moved diagonally across Kearney Road so that another wood frame building could be built on the chapel's original corner site in 1905. The original chapel still stands serving as the Sandy Hook Coast Guard's recreation center. (SHU.)

GYMNASIUM BUILDING NO. 70. The army justified building a gymnasium because Fort Hancock was an isolated post with limited recreation facilities. Capt. Moor Neilson Falls helped to complete the building on February 27, 1909. It included a four-lane bowling alley in the basement. When the adjacent YMCA added a new gymnasium in 1941, the post gymnasium was converted into the post exchange (PX). The PX served as the post's department store carrying both necessities and many luxury goods and operated a nearby gas station until 1973. The bowling alleys are still in the basement but are warped after many years of non-use. (SHU.)

DOUBLE COMPANY BARRACKS BUILDING NO. 74. In 1907, the war department decided to increase the Fort Hancock garrison from four to six companies of Coast Artillery. Also referred to as a double artillery barracks, the large, U-shaped building was built at the south end of Barracks Row. On April 17, 1908, Captain Falls once again contracted with a building contractor to construct this barracks. Work commenced on June 1, 1908, and progressed so rapidly that the barracks was completed on May 20, 1909. The barracks cost $86,130.43, and its capacity was 218 soldiers. (SHU.)

Five

WORLD WAR I TO WORLD WAR II

Battery "A," 57th Artillery, C. A. C.

BATTERY A, 57TH COAST ARTILLERY REGIMENT. On April 6, 1917, Congress declared war on Germany, and America entered World War I. Units were activated, organized, or sent to Fort Hancock for training. Where formerly there had been hundreds of soldiers, there were now thousands of men at Sandy Hook during 1917 and 1918. On December 7, 1917, the 57th Coast Artillery Regiment was ordered to be organized at Fort Hancock. Enlisted personnel were transferred, and a number of new draftees were organized to create the 57th regiment. Battery A poses proudly in front of the north end of the nine-gun battery in this view from 1918. (SHU.)

A 155MM GUN. The soldiers of the 57th Coast Artillery Regiment would not stay at Fort Hancock. The regiment of 1,888 officers and men broke camp early on May 9, 1918, and marched to the Fort Hancock wharf, where they boarded the troopship SS *Grand Republic* and went to France. The 57th Artillery manned tractor-drawn, six-inch guns on its arrival in France. The 155mm gun illustrated here was the weapon the regiment fought with in France commonly known in the American service as the Grande Puissance Filloux (GPF). (SHU.)

TRACTOR-DRAWN 155MM GUN. To move heavy artillery across the war-torn landscape of France during World War I, mechanized tractors were employed. Here a 155mm gun fitted with treads for better traction over natural ground is being field tested at the Aberdeen Proving Ground around 1918. After the war, the 155mm gun would become the most widely used of the mobile artillery pieces adopted for American coastal defense. (SHU.)

TWELVE-INCH MODEL 1918 RAILWAY MORTAR. During 1917, the U.S. Ordnance Department removed 150 12-inch mortars from coastal defense emplacements and depots, and designed a new railway carriage mount for them. These were planned to be used for artillery support along the western front in France, but the war ended before the mortars could be delivered. Here a 12-inch railway mortar is seen in classic camouflage paint at the Aberdeen Proving Ground around 1918. Most of these mobile railway mortars were stored at Fort Eustis, Virginia, and would eventually equip the 52nd Coast Artillery Railway Regiment. (SHU.)

EIGHT-INCH MODEL 1918 RAILWAY GUN. The army also planned to use eight-inch guns in France in 1917 on railway mounts. Like the 12-inch mortars, Model 1888, M1A1 rifles were available from coastal fortifications and reserve stocks. By the end of the war only 24 mounts had been completed, of which only three where sent overseas. A total of 37 railway mounts were completed and would end up being used by the 52nd Coast Artillery Regiment in the post-war years. Here an eight-inch railway mount is seen in classic camouflage paint at the Aberdeen Proving Ground around 1918. (SHU.)

THE 57TH COAST ARTILLERY HONOR GUARD. These three Battery A, 57th Coast Artillery Regiment soldiers are unidentified, but they are the battery's color guard and are posing with the nine-gun battery in the background in this 1918 photograph.

SGT. CHARLES KENNGOTT. When the United States entered World War I, the Fort Hancock garrison was reinforced with 13 companies of the 9th New York Coast Defense Command, a New York National Guard unit that was federalized and at the post since August 1917. During the winter of 1917–1918, these companies were redesignated different numbered companies, including the 15th Company. Here Charles Kenngott, a member of the 15th Company, poses in a pre-1912-style army uniform that includes a first class plotter and observer sleeve insignia. (SHU.)

TYPICAL WORLD WAR I TEMPORARY BARRACKS. With more soldiers and draftees arriving to expand the Fort Hancock garrison, more housing and support facilities were built to accommodate them. Housing became critical, especially when the 1,400-man 9th New York Coast Defense Command arrived at the post during the summer of 1917. A number of wooden cantonment areas were built near the batteries. Here is a typical World War I–era barracks that was built at Sandy Hook to house 66 soldiers. None of the wooden structures built at Fort Hancock survived, as they were demolished during the 1920s and early 1930s. (SHU.)

A WORLD WAR I SURVIVOR. The only Fort Hancock building constructed during World War I still existing today is this concrete storehouse. It was built in 1918 to store flammable materials like paint, kerosene, and the like. It was given building No. 79 on the Fort Hancock buildings list, and is located behind firehouse building No. 51 and workshop building No. 34. (SHU.)

PVT. 1ST CLASS ARMANDO MARINI. Armando Marini served in the 5th Company, Coast Defenses of Sandy Hook. In 1916, the six Coast Artillery Companies at Fort Hancock were redesignated the 1st, 2nd, 3rd, 4th, 5th, and 6th Companies, Fort Hancock, but on August 31, 1917, the war department issued an order in which Coast Artillery Companies would be known as "Coast Defenses of Sandy Hook" instead of Fort Hancock. The 5th Company manned Battery Peck. After World War I ended, many soldiers were discharged in 1919 including Marini, who was discharged that April. (SHU.).

WORLD WAR I–ERA LIBERTY ARMY TRUCK. There is no information about this photograph, but it was taken at Fort Hancock either during or just after World War I. It is a great view of one of the thousands of so-called "Liberty Trucks" that were built in America to support the war here at home and overseas. The truck was probably operated by the Motor Transport or Quartermaster Corps, and is seen here parked in front of quartermaster storehouse building No. 32, which is behind the truck. (SHU.)

LOADING BATTERY KINGMAN. By World War I, foreign battleships could fire their main battery guns in high arcs from over 15 miles offshore. This technical improvement in naval weaponry made disappearing guns obsolete. To counter the threat of high-angle, long-range naval fire, the U.S. Army Ordnance Department introduced the Model 1917 barbette gun carriage, seen here being readied for test firing at Battery Kingman in June 1919. (SHU.)

TEST FIRING BATTERY KINGMAN. Army engineers built two 12-inch model barbette gun batteries near the south end of Horseshoe Cove during 1917. Each battery had two 12-inch guns, each mounted on a large circular concrete gun platform. The guns and carriages were not mounted until February 1919, and in June the guns were test fired, which is happening here at Battery Kingman. (SHU.)

TWELVE-INCH GUN BREECH, CLOSED. Close up, the back end of this Model 1895, M1A4, 12-inch gun at Battery Kingman does not look big, but it was, weighing 52 tons and measuring 37.6 feet in length. The breechblock is in closed position. The four round objects at the top and bottom of the gun are recoil cylinders, which were long steel liquid-filled tubes that slowed down the gun barrel's recoil (kick back) when it fired. (SHU.)

TWELVE-INCH GUN BREECH, OPEN. The soldiers have now opened the breechblock, allowing a view down inside the rifled bore of the Model 1895 gun at Battery Kingman. Again, the long gun barrel looks short in the photograph, but this is an optical illusion. The battery was named in honor of Brig. Gen. Dan C. Kingman, chief of army engineers, who died in November 1916. Located south of Battery Kingman, Battery Mills was named after Albert L. Mills, a Spanish-American War Medal of Honor winner. (SHU.)

LOOKING SOUTH FROM KINGMAN TOWARD MILLS. This 1940 or 1941 photograph was taken from atop the sand and earthen-covered traverse of Battery Kingman looking towards Battery Mills (top center) and south down Sandy Hook. The Atlantic Ocean is in the left background, and Horseshoe Cove is to the right. The wooden building at right is a non-commissioned officer's quarters, as someone was needed to be present on site since these batteries were about two miles from the main post. (SHU.)

LOOKING SOUTH FROM MILLS TOWARD KINGMAN. This is another image from the same time period, but now the view is looking north with Battery Mills number two gun emplacement in the foreground and Battery Kingman in the distance (top center). The ocean is to the right, and Horseshoe Cove is at upper left along with a railroad bed that supplied the batteries. The army engineers choose this site on the bay side so that the batteries would be hidden from view from the ocean side by the maritime forest of holly and cedar trees located down the center of Sandy Hook. (SHU.)

ENTRANCE INTO TRAVERSE OF BATTERY KINGMAN. Each pair of guns at Batteries Kingman and Mills had a large traverse located between them. Each traverse was, in effect, a massive concrete blockhouse which had magazines, storerooms, a generator room, and latrines inside and was covered with earth and sand to resemble a large hill. The north and south ends of each traverse had these large entrances, which allowed army railroad cars access inside to deliver ammunition and supplies. (SHU.)

BATTERY KINGMAN'S NUMBER TWO BARBETTE GUN. If one looked at the traverse mentioned above and then turned around, one would see this 12-inch barbette mounted gun on its circular concrete platform, which allowed the gun to fire over 20 miles in any direction. This meant that it could hit lower Manhattan in New York City. This is Battery Kingman's north gun emplacement, number two, with Sandy Hook's holly and cedar forest in the background in the late 1930s. (SHU.)

AMMUNITION CARTS AT BATTERY KINGMAN. This excellent view shows how ammunition was brought out of the traverses to the guns at batteries Kingman and Mills. Here four ammunition carts have been lined up for the photograph sometime in the early 1920s. The army called these carts "Ammunition Trucks: A steerable three-wheeled truck, with suitable space for carrying a complete charge from the delivery or reserve table to the breech of cannon." During a gun drill, one truck would carry a projectile to the gun closely followed by another with a bagged powder charge. (SHU.)

RAMMING IN A 12-INCH PROJECTILE. A half-ton projectile is about to be rammed into the breech of a 12-inch gun at Battery Kingman around 1941. To load and fire the gun, 37 soldiers, known as the gun section, were required, three of which are seen here. The soldiers had numbers, and number four is seen at right holding the breechblock open during loading. The soldiers at left are numbers one and two, who also assisted in loading and closing the breechblock. (SHU.)

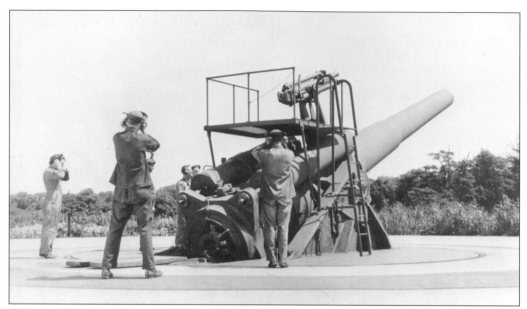

BATTERY KINGMAN READY FOR FIRING. In this 1941 view, the 12-inch gun at Battery Kingman is ready for firing. The three soldiers are bracing themselves for the tremendous concussion (shock wave) that will come out of the gun when it is fired. To counter the concussion's pressure, these soldiers were taught to open their mouths, raise their feet and cup their hands over their ears. The platform over the gun holds a 75mm gun that was used in place of firing the 12-inch gun to save wear and tear on the rifling grooves inside the larger gun. (SHU.)

FIRE CONTROL TOWER. With the introduction of 12- and 16-inch barbette mounted guns during World War I, the Coast Artillery Corps had weapons capable of firing from 20 to 28 miles but now needed to sight targets at greater distances. For the 1919 firing tests of Batteries Kingman and Mills, the army experimented with using observation balloons. Two steel girder battery commander station towers were also built to help sight targets for Batteries Kingman and Mills. In the end, the army chose to go with tall fire control towers instead of observation balloons to sight their long-range guns. The tower seen here, along with an identical tower out of view to the right, stood along the west side of Atlantic Drive. Their concrete footings still remain scattered in the dunes and underbrush next to Atlantic Drive. (SHU.)

GUNNISON TOWER. By the 1930s, fire control towers were 100-feet tall and resembled forest fire spotting towers. This is Gunnison Tower, so named because it stood a few hundred yards west of Battery Gunnison. However it actually sighted targets for Battery Harris, a 16-inch gun battery located at Fort Tilden on Breezy Point across the harbor entrance from Sandy Hook. The tower was used through World War II and then demolished in the immediate post-war years. (SHU.)

CITIZENS' MILITARY TRAINING CAMP. After World War I, the National Defense Act of June 4, 1920, advocated a citizen army. Fort Hancock would play a role in training citizen soldiers who would back up the small regular U.S. Army. Young men could attend the Citizens Military Training Camps (CMTC) for a month during the summer without actually enlisting in the army. The primary objective was to instruct and train warrant officers, enlisted men, and civilians in military instruction and athletics. The first camps were organized in 1921 and at Fort Hancock continued through the 1930s. Officers Row is mostly hidden by shade trees. (SHU.)

PUMP HOUSE BUILDING NO. 37. This lowly sewerage pump house is shown here to illustrate the big budget cutbacks the country endured during the 1920s after World War I. The army built only five buildings around Fort Hancock during the 1920s, and four of those were built between 1921 and 1922 before military funding was cut back. This pump house was built in 1928 and is still at Fort Hancock doing the job it was designed to do many years ago. It illustrates the fact that the "roaring twenties" may have been "boom" times for the civilian world, but it was "bust" times for military budgets as far as the army was concerned. (SHU.)

PUMP HOUSE BUILDING NO. 37 DURING HURRICANE DONNA. This photograph is quite a contrast to the one showing pump house building No. 37 high and dry on a nice day. It is used here to show that Fort Hancock could be flooded during a fierce nor'easter or hurricane. This view was taken from the front porch of Officer's Row quarters No. 6 during Hurricane Donna in 1960 to illustrate the fact that parts of Fort Hancock have flooded during storms. (SHU.)

CONSTRUCTING THE NEW MINE CASEMATE. The construction of a new protected mining casemate is going on in this 1921 view. This originally had been the dynamite gun battery where three guns, two of 15-inch caliber and one of eight-inch caliber, were mounted in a row in 1889 in the courtyard ground seen here. The guns fired projectiles loaded with volatile TNT by using compressed steam to fire the projectiles instead of using gunpowder, the violent explosion of which would blow up the TNT-filled projectiles while inside the guns. The dynamite gun battery met with limited success and was dismantled in 1901. (SHU.)

EARTHWORK SLOPE OF THE MINE CASEMATE. This is the outside north sand slope of the former dynamite gun battery facing north toward New York Harbor. The crane is busy converting the east wall facing the ocean into Fort Hancock's new protected mining casemate. The small white hut in front of the crane is an interesting feature especially with that long pipe sticking out of it. (SHU.)

THREE-INCH AAA GUN ATOP THE MINE CASEMATE. The pipe that was seen sticking out of the white hut in the lower photograph on page 105 is seen here close up. It is actually the barrel of a three-inch antiaircraft gun that is stored in its protective shelter. This was one of two three-inch antiaircraft guns that were emplaced on top of the former dynamite gun battery in 1920 or 1921. (SHU.)

UNDERWATER MINE EXPLODING. The explosion of an army controlled mine full of 100 or 200 pounds of TNT is well illustrated here. If an enemy ship was passing over this mine when it detonated, the ship would most probably be destroyed and if passing close by, it would be heavily damaged. Underwater mines were a big but unseen and unsung part of America's harbor defenses from the 1890s through World War II. (SHU.)

AERIAL VIEW OF FORT HANCOCK. In this scenic aerial view taken between World War I and World War II, Fort Hancock almost resembles a quiet, rustic-looking Victorian-era college campus. The kidney-shaped main parade field stretches from the lower left to the center of the photograph, with the hospital at lower left, Officers Row fronting Sandy Hook Bay, the big U-shaped barracks building No. 74, the rest of Barracks Row and Sergeants Row, and the white Sandy Hook Lighthouse at middle right. The tip of Sandy Hook is out of view, just above the Fort Hancock docks at top center. (SHU.)

BATTERY C, 52ND COAST ARTILLERY ON PARADE. With their guidons (pennant flags) flapping in the breeze, Battery C, 52nd Coast Artillery (Railway) Regiment, marches smartly and proudly across the main parade field on an Army Day parade in this classic view around 1940 or 1941. This scene is a vestige of the small U.S. Army, which before America entered World War II, was known as "the old army," an army of long-serving soldiers who made up "the regulars" and who would form the core of, and provide the leadership for, a greatly expanded army during and long after World War II. (SHU.)

EIGHT-INCH RAILWAY GUN READY TO FIRE. About midway down the Sandy Hook peninsula between Fort Hancock and Sandy Hook's south end was a sand dune area fronting the ocean. Here railroad spurs ran into the back dune area off the main army railroad line. This was where the 52nd Coast Artillery's Battery E fired their eight-inch railway guns, and Battery C fired their 12-inch railway mortars for their annual target practice. Here an eight-inch railway gun is getting ready to fire in 1939 or 1940. (SHU.)

EIGHT-INCH RAILWAY GUN FIRING. At the command "Fire!" an eight-inch railway gun belches forth exploding gunpowder and smoke as it sends an eight-inch, 260-pound armor-piercing projectile streaking at 2,750 feet per second toward a towed target several miles offshore. Albin Zwiazek recalled: "Battery E set up their 8-inch guns for firing right next to us, Battery C, who had 12-inch mortars. Each battery had 4 guns. Boy, those 8-inch guns, they had a large 'crack' sound to them! They were very bad on the ears!" (SHU.)

TWELVE-INCH RAILWAY MORTAR READY TO FIRE. In this 1931 view, a Battery C, 52nd Coast Artillery, mortar crew readies a Model 1890, 12-inch railway mortar for firing under the careful eye of two officers standing at right. Note the C Battery, 52nd guidon insignia painted on the side of the loading platform and the overhead trolley bridge for transporting a 12-inch projectile from the ammunition boxcar partially seen at left. (SHU.)

TWELVE-INCH RAILWAY MORTAR FIRING. This 12-inch railway mortar has just fired its half-ton armor-piercing projectile high into the sky, and its outrigger arms press into the sand, some of which can be seen flying slightly into the air. These railway mortars had a maximum elevation of 65 degrees and range of about 8.5 miles. Albin Zwiazek remembered: "When a 12-inch mortar fired, it wasn't as bad as those 8-inch guns, it made a big loud 'BOOM' sound. But those 8-inch guns, they made a big 'CRACK' sound, because their barrels were longer then mortars. Remember, 'the longer the barrel, the sharper the crack.'" (SHU.)

A FAMOUS VISITOR, COL. CHARLES LINDBERG. On August 2, 1939, Albin Zwiazek, Battery C, 52nd Coast Artillery, was standing on the wooden observation deck. He recalls that "two men in civilian suits came walking up to the platform. There was a water bucket near the platform for the soldiers to drink from, and I heard one of my fellow soldiers standing near the bucket say 'Would the Colonel care for a drink of water?' Then I realized who it was. The famous aviator, Charles Lindbergh, had showed up with a friend at the invitation of the commanding officer of Fort Hancock to watch the target practice being conducted at Sandy Hook." (SHU.)

THE 52ND COAST ARTILLERY GUN PARK. The 52nd Coast Artillery's guns, mortars, and boxcars (containing ammunition, a plotting room, radio and telephone communications, and a field kitchen) were stored at the "gun park," seen here around 1937. This originally was where new gun barrels were stacked on the concrete wall while awaiting testing at the Sandy Hook Proving Ground. The innocent-looking hill in the photograph (top left) is actually the protective earthwork slope at the south end of the nine-gun battery. Today this site is part of North Beach, a popular bathing-beach area. (SHU.)

TOP SECRET RADAR TESTING SITE. This is the field laboratory building built by Fort Monmouth's U.S. Army Signal Corps personnel in 1937 for the top secret testing of radio position finding equipment known as radar (radio detecting and ranging). Fort Monmouth personnel wanted to use Sandy Hook for radar testing because it was isolated and secured and no one would be able to see the radar equipment being tested. This view, taken November 3, 1941, is looking south with the Navesink Highlands in the background. Today all the buildings are gone, and this area is known as Fishing Beach, a poplar fishing spot. (SHU.)

SIGNAL CORPS RADAR 268 RADAR ANTENNA. Here is a Signal Corps Radar No. 268 (SCR-268 Radar) antenna being tested at Sandy Hook around 1941. In the top photograph, look closely at the right of the lab building where a partially assembled SCR-268 radio set antenna can be seen. The SCR-268 was the U.S. Army's first radar system. Sandy Hook made an excellent place to test radar waves on passing airplanes and ships where the radar units were hidden from view far from the local mainland. Hundreds of SCR-268, SCR-270, and SCR-271 units were tested at Sandy Hook and then used by the army around the world to help win World War II. (SHU.)

THOSE GOOD OLD ARMY MULES. Civilian Conservation Corps (CCC) worker Mike Lakomie is seen here in 1937, mounted on one of the army mules used on the post for labor duty. Mike recalled that "mules were used to haul the mowing tractors around the post to mow all of those lawns. No motor powered mowers back then." Fellow CCC worker George Haas remembered that "one of the army mules was named 'Rasmus.' Now that mule was real smart. Whenever the bugler blew the chow call for lunch that darn mule KNEW the sound of the call, and no matter what he was doing at that time, he would just turn around and go right back to the stables building to eat his lunch!" (SHU.)

A HARD WORKING CCC BOY. Here CCC boy Mike Lakomie jokes for the camera in August 1936 by one of the Rodman gun lawn ornaments across from officers' quarters No. 12. Lakomie said, "I'm making believe I'm slacking off and not doing any work, but let me tell you, they worked us very hard at Sandy Hook. We clear cut much of the wooded areas and cleaned a lot of debris washing up on the beaches. We dug ditches. We build sidewalks. We did a lot of work on many of the fort buildings. We hand shoveled snow off the streets, sidewalks, and even the railroad tracks out here. We did everything you can think of." (SHU.)

"CCC Boy" Andy Diano Posing with Anne Sheperd. Anne Sheperd was the daughter of Capt. Charles Sheperd, and is seen here in front of Officers Row quarters No. 1 around 1936. Andy Diano recalled that "we were building new clay double tennis courts next to quarters No. 1. It was a very hot day and little Anne Sheperd was playing there by the house. Her nursemaid gave us cold lemonade. Anne was such a nice little girl. Captain Sheperd later left Fort Hancock and went to Fort Monroe, Virginia, and I never say Anne again." (SHU.)

Scotland Trail Gazebo. The rustic looking gazebo was at the east end of Scotland Trail, which was built by CCC Company 288 around 1937. The trail was so named because it ended at this gazebo, which was in line with and opposite the Scotland Lightship anchored several miles offshore. In 1866, two ships collided off Sandy Hook. The captain of one ship named *Scotland*, ordered the ship toward Sandy Hook where he hoped he could reach shallow water so the ship could later be salvaged. Unfortunately the *Scotland* sank, and a lightship was placed over the wreck, which eventually was designated Scotland Lightship.

CCC BOYS BUILDING THE 20-INCH RODMAN GUN NUMBER TWO BASE. For many years since 1903, when Fort Hancock got the gun transferred from the Sandy Hook Proving Ground, the rare 20-inch Rodman gun number two sat on the lawn on blocks opposite firehouse building No. 51. CCC Company 288 was assigned the task of making a new concrete base to mount the gun barrel. Here the CCC boys are building the concrete base around 1937 in front of the west end of stables building No. 36. Their foreman on this job was Sgt. Louis Rasga, who had been a body bearer for the Unknown Soldier in Washington, D.C., on November 11, 1921. (SHU.)

NEWLY COMPLETED 20-INCH RODMAN GUN NUMBER TWO BASE. The original location of the concrete base mounting the 20-inch Rodman gun number two was on South Bragg Drive where it intersected with Kearney Road. The World War I concrete storehouse building No. 79 can be seen just to the right of the gun's muzzle, and at far right is the corner of firehouse building No. 51 showing its tower used to dry fire hoses after use. A special muzzle cover was made for the gun when the base was made, which shows the insignia of the U.S. Army Ordnance Department. (SHU.)

TWENTY-INCH RODMAN GUN NUMBER TWO AND BASE AT ITS NEW LOCATION. This 1938 or 1939 picture, taken by John Bishop, shows that the new concrete base and 20-inch Rodman gun number two were somehow moved about 100 feet from where the base was built halfway between the stables building (on the left) and the firehouse. The firehouse's hose tower is visible over the back of the gun. Mike Lakomie said, "You know, I helped build that concrete base and mount the gun on it, but I just don't remember how or who moved it from where we built the base and mounted the gun over to that little triangular piece of land where it sits today." (SHU.)

USS TUCKER AT HORSESHOE COVE. Named after Capt. Samuel Tucker, a navy veteran of the American Revolution and the War of 1812, this Destroyer was commissioned on April 11, 1916, and designated Destroyer No. 57. During World War I the USS *Tucker* hunted German submarines, escorted and convoyed allied ships in war zones, and provided assistance to ships in distress. During Prohibition, the Destroyer was transferred to the U.S. Coast Guard and designated CG-23, where it joined the "rum patrol" and chased rumrunners while attempting to enforce prohibition laws. The former USS *Tucker* finally ended her days serving as a Sea Scout training ship, seen here docked at Horseshoe Cove in Sandy Hook in 1936. (SHU.)

CCC Boys Building the Halyburton Monument. CCC Company 288 built a new monument to commemorate the ill-fated Halyburton detachment that died at Horseshoe Cove in 1783. Here N. Deats (left) and Mike Lakomie (right) have the monument about half completed in May 1937. Mike Lakomie remembered, "Our CCC camp was over in the right background in the photo. I don't remember any plans or drawings, we just built the monument as we went along. We used a local stone that people called 'peanut stone' or 'peanut brittle stone' because it was brown colored, had a lot of little pebbles and stones in it, and was brittle and broke apart rather easily when you hit it." (SHU.)

CCC Boy Mike Lakomie Posing With the Halyburton Monument. This photograph, dated August 28, 1937, shows Mike Lakomie posing proudly with the newly completed Halyburton Monument. Mike Lakomie recalled, "I was very proud to have built the monument. I'm wearing my CCC uniform just for this picture. Notice that there is no bronze plaque on the monument in this picture. I left the CCC at the end of the summer of 1937, and when I left there was still no plaque on the monument, so they must have put the plaque on it sometime after I left." (SHU.)

HALYBURTON MEMORIAL PARK. This view shows that the grounds around the Halyburton Monument were eventually landscaped, probably sometime during the fall of 1937 and the spring or summer of 1938, when CCC Company 288 left Sandy Hook. Note the front of the large balloon hangar at the upper left. This large metal structure had been built in 1921 to house army observation balloons to spot targets for Fort Hancock's long-range guns but, as it turned out, this never happened. CCC Company 288's camp was located behind the trees seen in the background. (SHU.)

HALYBURTON MONUMENT WITH PLAQUE. The monument's plaque states that "On this spot were buried the remains of the Honorable Hamilton Douglas Halyburton, 1st Lieutenant, Royal Navy . . . [along with] James Champion, Lieutenant of Marines. Together with twelve members of the crew of HMS Assistance who died here at Sandy Hook in line of Duty on December 31, 1783. Erected and Dedicated in 1939." Actually Capt. Moor Neilson Falls reported that the remains were found several hundred feet away to the northwest. Also the monument was not erected in 1939 but in 1937. It probably was dedicated in 1939, as the king and queen of England visited that June. (SHU.)

ALBIN ZWIAZEK AND THE MORNING INSPECTION AT BARRACKS NO. 74. Serving in Battery C, 52nd Coast Artillery Regiment, Railway, Albin Zwiazek served at Fort Hancock from February 1937 to February 1940. On the top left is a picture of him in 1937, and on the top right he is pictured in the spring of 1939. The bottom photograph is a picture taken by CCC worker Mike Lakomie early one August morning in 1937. (SHU.)

OFFICERS CLUB FIRE, APRIL 9, 1938. This stately brick building with a mansard roof was completed in 1879. It served as the officers' quarters at the Sandy Hook Proving Ground from 1879 to 1919. Fort Hancock took over more than 100 buildings when the proving ground closed and used it to house up to four married officers and their families. In 1936, the building became the Fort Hancock Officers Club. The building caught fire in 1917 but was saved by ordnance personnel. On April 9, 1938, the officers club caught fire again. (SHU.)

BATTERY E, 52ND COAST ARTILLERY GUARD OF HONOR. Battery E was chosen to be the guard of honor when their Royal Majesties King George VI and Queen Elizabeth of England stopped at Red Bank, while on their way from Washington, D.C., to New York City via Sandy Hook. Battery E is seen here getting ready to greet the monarchs at the Red Bank Railroad Station on the morning of June 10, 1939. Because war was threatening in Europe, security was tight, and the royal motorcade traveled quickly to Sandy Hook. The destroyer USS *Warrington* (DD-383) was waiting at the Fort Hancock docks for the royal couple. (SHU.)

PRES. FRANKLIN D. ROOSEVELT ARRIVES AT FORT HANCOCK. On August 24, 1939, as Germany was threatening to invade Poland, Pres. Franklin D. Roosevelt made a dramatic gesture for peace. The president cut short a vacation cruise on the cruiser USS *Tuscaloosa* (CA-37) and transferred to the destroyer USS *Lang* (DD-399), which took Roosevelt and his party to the Fort Hancock wharf, seen arriving here. The *Lang* was named after seaman John Lang of New Brunswick, New Jersey, who fought in the War of 1812. The destroyer was built at the Federal Shipbuilding and Dry Dock Company in Kearny, was commissioned March 30, 1939, and received 11 battle stars for its World War II service. (SHU.)

ROOSEVELT AT THE FORT HANCOCK DOCK. As the president disembarked from the USS *Lang* onto the dock, he was welcomed by a Coast Artillery guard of honor and a 21-gun salute. Security was tight and the presidential party quickly left the post. As the presidential party drove down Sandy Hook en route to the Red Bank railroad station, another 21-gun salute was fired. When Roosevelt arrived in Washington, D.C., later that day, he officially asked Germany, Italy, and Poland to negotiate their differences, but his effort was in vain. On September 1, 1939, Germany invaded Poland and started World War II. (SHU.)

TENT CITY. As war raged in Europe during 1940, America remained neutral. However, to prepare the country for war, Roosevelt ordered state National Guard units into federal service and called up a number of reserves. The 245th New York National Guard Regiment had just completed its annual summer training at Fort Hancock when the president federalized the unit in mid-September 1940, making the unit the 245th Coast Artillery Regiment. To accommodate the entire regiment, a tent city, which would become a familiar sight at military installations all across America, was established at Fort Hancock. (SHU.)

NEW BARRACKS AT CAMP LOW. Looking north, wooden barracks and mess halls can be seen being constructed by contractors in this view from 1940 or 1941. The long rectangular one-story building seen at right is one of the CCC camp barracks built in 1935. The large metal building seen at far right is the observation balloon storage hangar built in 1921. Off to the left out of the photograph is Horseshoe Cove. This entire area was known as Camp Low, presumably because this area, used as encampment area since at least the 1890s, was located by the low, marshy area of Horseshoe Cove. Note the Halyburton monument just left of the center in the photograph. (SHU.)

CONDUCTING TARGET PRACTICE WITH A 155MM GUN CREW. The 155mm gun was adopted for mobile seacoast defense after World War I. It was an Americanized version of a 1917 French army design and was known at the Model 1918 in the U.S. Army. The 155mm gun pictured here between 1938 and 1941 was still a mainstay coast artillery weapon when America entered World War II and would remain so throughout most of that war. (SHU.)

DISAPPEARING RAILWAY SEARCHLIGHT. Searchlights were not confined to fixed positions as can be seen here. This is a disappearing searchlight tower mounted on a railroad flat car. Col. Henry Neri commanded the searchlight battery in the 245th Coast Artillery regiment during World War II. Neri remembered, "We had some of these disappearing searchlights mounted on railway cars. Let me tell you, my boys, and they were just young boys back then, risked life and limb serving on those searchlight towers. And on those railway cars, on damp, rainy, or cold freezing nights, you could easily slip and fall off, and that would be it!" (SHU.)

AAA GUN ON **T**OP OF THE **F**ORMER **M**ORTAR **B**ATTERY. Lt. Brian P. Emerson, Battery B, 245th Coast Artillery Regiment, is instructing newly inducted "selectees" (recently drafted men) on the working of a Model 1917 three-inch antiaircraft gun mount about 1941. This was one of three of these types of antiaircraft guns that were placed on top of the former mortar battery in 1921 to add antiaircraft defense for Fort Hancock. In 1940–1941 these emplacements were designated AAA Gun Battery No. 2, and would serve through World War II. (SHU.)

AAA GUN **D**RILL. The shout of "Gas!" makes these Battery B, 245th Coast Artillery soldiers break out their gas masks quickly while manning a Model 1917 three-inch antiaircraft gun at AAA Gun Battery No. 2 atop the former mortar battery. Note one of the other three AAA guns in the left background in this photograph from 1940 or 1941. Today this entire area is heavily overgrown with vegetation. (SHU.)

THE COVERED PASSAGE. This close-up view showed the covered passage connecting into the southwest corner of barracks building No. 74, which would serve as an auxiliary hospital from 1941 through 1945. This interesting structure was demolished soon after World War II ended. (SHU.)

SOLDIERS MANNING A MACHINE GUN. In this c. 1941 publicity shot, two members of the 245th Coast Artillery man a water-cooled .50 caliber machine gun. An interesting feature seen in the background is the long covered passage that was constructed in 1941. It connected the post hospital with the southwest corner of barracks building No. 74 (left), which was converted into an auxiliary hospital in January 1941. Hospital staff, patients, and visitors would be protected from the weather by walking inside this interesting but long-gone structure. (SHU.)

INSIDE THE BOMBPROOF. The tunnel system inside the former mortar Batteries McCook and Reynolds took on another important mission when they were converted into a Harbor Defense Command Post (HDCP) around 1940 or 1941. The HDCP served as a centralized command headquarters to coordinate the defense of lower New York Harbor between Forts Hancock, Tilden, Hamilton, and Wadsworth. This is an early publicity shot inside the HDCP, but after America entered World War II, the tunnel system here was extensively renovated and became a very important part of defending New York Harbor from sea and air attacks. (SHU.)

Obsolete but beautiful.

OBSOLETE BUT BEAUTIFUL. As the sun sets over Sandy Hook Bay, a CMTC trainee poses by one of the old eight-inch Rodman guns located in front of Officers Row quarters No. 12. On this photograph, from 1939 or 1940, the young CMTC trainee wrote "Obsolete but beautiful." He was correct in that. As America headed toward World War II, the old smoothbore, muzzle-loading Rodman seen here was long obsolete, but so were the disappearing guns of Fort Hancock. However, Fort Hancock would soon be headed towards the busiest and most important period in its history. (SHU.)

ACROSS AMERICA, PEOPLE ARE DISCOVERING SOMETHING WONDERFUL. *THEIR HERITAGE.*

Arcadia Publishing is the leading local history publisher in the United States. With more than 3,000 titles in print and hundreds of new titles released every year, Arcadia has extensive specialized experience chronicling the history of communities and celebrating America's hidden stories, bringing to life the people, places, and events from the past. To discover the history of other communities across the nation, please visit:

www.arcadiapublishing.com

Customized search tools allow you to find regional history books about the town where you grew up, the cities where your friends and family live, the town where your parents met, or even that retirement spot you've been dreaming about.